CHRISTIAN PUBLISHING HOUSE & PROBE MINISTRIES

TECHNOLOGY AND SOCIAL TRENDS
A Biblical Point of View

KERBY ANDERSON

Like Israel in the days of David, 'are we ones who have an understanding of the times, to know what we as Christians ought to do?'—1 Chron 12:32.

TECHNOLOGY AND SOCIAL TRENDS

A Biblical Point of View

Kerby Anderson

Christian Publishing House
Cambridge, Ohio

Copyright © 2016 Kerby Anderson

All rights reserved. Except for brief quotations in articles, other publications, book reviews, and blogs, no part of this book may be reproduced in any manner without prior written permission from the publishers. For information, write,

support@christianpublishers.org

Unless otherwise stated, Scripture quotations are from *New American Standard Bible (NASB)* Copyright © 1960, 1962, 1963, 1968, 1971, 1972, 1973, 1975, 1977, **1995** by The Lockman Foundation

TECHNOLOGY AND SOCIAL TRENDS: A Biblical Point of View by Kerby Anderson

ISBN-13: 978-1-945757-29-7

ISBN-10: 1-945757-29-9

Table of Contents

Kerby Anderson 1

Preface 2

SECTION 1 TECHNOLOGY 4

How is technology affecting me? How should I use digital technology wisely? Do I become excessively distressed, possibly even upset, when I am unable to access the Internet or use my electronic device? Am I losing sleep because I am unable to stop checking my messages? Is my use of technology causing me to ignore my family? 4

CHAPTER 1 Technological Challenges in the 21st Century 5

Theology of Technology 5

The Challenge of Biotechnology 8

The Challenge of Information Technology 16

Technology and Human Nature 20

CHAPTER 2 The Challenge of Transhumanism 23

Transhumanism in the Movies 24

Biblical Perspective 26

CHAPTER 3 Globalization and the Internet .. 28

Challenge of the Internet 29

Internet Regulation 30

Government and Intermediaries 32

Globalization and Government 33

CHAPTER 4 Big Data and Big Brother 36

Big Data 36

Big Brother 39

CHAPTER 5 Privacy and Homeland Security . 45

A Supersnoop's Dream 45

The Patriot Act 46

Immigration Threats 48

History of Governmental Power 50

Christian Perspective on Government and Privacy 51

CHAPTER 6 Sins of Privacy 54

SECTION 2 SOCIAL TRENDS 58

How is this rapidly changing world affecting me? What type of technological entertainment should I choose? How will this technology affect me personally and my relationship with God? How are these trends affecting my generation? Do these new technological trends help or harm my family? 58

CHAPTER 7 The Changing American Family . 59

Conflicting Attitudes about Marriage and Family 61

Changing Trends in Marriage 63

Changing Trends in Family 66

CHAPTER 8 Exponential Times 70

Exponential Growth 72

Warnings About Exponential Growth 74

Information Explosion 76

Exponential Times and a Biblical Worldview 78

CHAPTER 9 Baby Boomerangs 80

Seekers of Experiences 82

Boomers, Busters, and Their Children 83
Skeptical of Society 85
Spiritual Hunger... 87

CHAPTER 10 Midlife Transition 90
The Age 40 Transition 91
The Seasons of a Man's Life.............................. 93
New Roles... 95
Mortality.. 96
Culminating Events 97
Intense Introspection 97
Leaving a Legacy... 98
Application.. 99

CHAPTER 11 Time and Busyness.................... 101
The Technology of Time...................................101
Time-Controlling Devices................................ 103
No Time to Talk... 104
Never Enough Time... 106
Redeeming the Time..108

CHAPTER 12 Loneliness 110
Marriage Patterns 111
Living-Together Loneliness 113
Male Loneliness 115
Crowded Loneliness...117

CHAPTER 13 The Millennial Generation 120
Motivating the Millennials 123

Millennials and Media 125

Millennials and Religion 127

CHAPTER 14 Sex and Violence on Television 129

The Extent of the Problem................................129

Television's Impact on Behavior 133

Sex on Television 134

Violence on Television 136

Biblical Perspective 138

CHAPTER 15 Kids Killing Kids 141

The Media and Video Games 142

Violence and Teenage Rebellion 144

Tolerance..146

Spiritual Issues 148

CHAPTER 16 Video Games........................... 151

Grand Theft Auto... 151

Benefits of Video Games..................................152

Types of Video Games 155

Violent Video Games 156

Biblical Discernment 159

CHAPTER 17 Media and Discernment 161

Media Exposure 161

Biblical Discernment 163

Worldview of the News Media 164

Biblical Principles and Application....................168

Bibliography 170

Other Books by Kerby Anderson 172

Kerby Anderson

Kerby Anderson is the President of Probe Ministries. He holds master's degrees from Yale University (science) and Georgetown University (government).

He also serves as a visiting professor at Dallas Theological Seminary and has spoken on dozens of university campuses including University of Michigan, Vanderbilt University, Princeton University, Johns Hopkins University, University of Colorado and University of Texas.

He is the author of sixteen books including *Signs of Warning*, *Signs of Hope*, *Moral Dilemmas*, *Christian Ethics in Plain Language*, *A Biblical Point of View on Islam*, *A Biblical Point of View on Homosexuality*, *A Biblical Point of View on Intelligent Design*, *A Biblical Point of View on Spiritual Warfare*, and *Managing Your Money in Tough Times*. He is also the editor of many books including: *Marriage, Family, & Sexuality* and *Technology, Spirituality, & Social Trends*.

He is the host of "Point of View" radio talk show and regular guest on "Fire Away" (American Family Radio). He has appeared or numerous radio and TV talk shows including the "MacNeil/Lehrer News Hour," "Focus on the Family," "Beverly LaHaye Live," and "The 700 Club."

He produces a daily syndicated radio commentary and writes editorials that have appeared in the *Dallas Morning News*, the *Miami Herald*, the *San Jose Mercury*, and the *Houston Post*. His radio commentaries have been syndicated by International Media Services, United Press International, American Family Radio, Moody Radio, and the USA Radio Network.

Kerby is married to Susanne and is the father of three grown children.

Preface

We are living in the midst of remarkable technological innovation and social change. We are facing significant challenges in the area of technology. We are losing our privacy as big data and big government work together to create big brother. Each generation (baby boomers, baby busters, and millennials) is facing social and demographic challenges.

Predicting the future is difficult. After World War I the European nations assumed that the peace treaty would guarantee that Germany would not reemerge. Twenty years later it looked like Germany would dominate the world. By the 1960s, Germany was split down the middle, and the challenge was the Cold War between the two superpowers of Russia and the United States. By the 1990s, the Soviet Union collapsed, leaving the US as the sole superpower. Then came September 11, 2001, that focused our country and the world on Muslim terrorism. Just about the time we think we know what the future holds, the world changes.

Nevertheless, there are trends that we can see and understand. Jesus admonished those around Him because they could not "read the signs of the times" (Matthew 16:3). The future is difficult to predict and "we see in a mirror dimly" (1 Cor. 13:12). That should not prevent us from watching and evaluating the trends that are unfolding before us.

The following chapters first aired as Probe radio programs, and some of them were collected in the earlier book: *Technology, Spirituality, & Social Trends* (Grand Rapids, MI: Kregel, 2002). The first section examines the technological challenges we face (bioethics, information revolution, privacy). The second section provides an overview of the many social trends affecting our faith, family, and freedom.

We need to discern the signs and understand our world. Of all the men surrounding King David, it was the sons of Issachar who "understood the times, with knowledge of what Israel should do" (1 Chron. 12:32). Likewise, we need to understand our times with knowledge of what Christians should do.

SECTION 1 TECHNOLOGY

How is technology affecting me? How should I use digital technology wisely? Do I become excessively distressed, possibly even upset, when I am unable to access the Internet or use my electronic device? Am I losing sleep because I am unable to stop checking my messages? Is my use of technology causing me to ignore my family?

CHAPTER 1 Technological Challenges in the 21st Century

We live in historical times. And we will face new challenges as we enter the 21st century, especially in the area of technology. The fields of biotechnology and information technology have the capacity to change the social landscape and even alter the way we make ethical decisions. These are not challenges for the faint-hearted. We must bring a tough- minded Christianity into the 21st century.

We are reminded in 1 Chronicles 12:32 (NIV) that the men of Issachar "understood the times and knew what Israel should do." Likewise, we must understand our times and know what we should do. New ethical challenges await us as we consider the moral issues of our day and begin to analyze them from a biblical perspective.

We should also enter into the task with humility. We should not make the mistake of thinking that we can accurately see into the future. However, we can analyze trends and look at new inventions and begin to see the implications of these remarkable changes. Our challenge will always be to apply the timeless truths of Scripture to the quickly changing world around us.

How should Christians analyze the technological changes taking place? First, we must begin by developing a theology of technology.

Theology of Technology

Technology is really nothing more than the systematic modification of the environment for human ends. This might be a process or activity that extends or enhances a human function. A telescope extends man's visual perception. A tractor extends one's physical ability. A computer extends a person's ability to calculate.

The biblical mandate for developing and using technology is stated in Genesis 1:28. God gave mankind dominion over the land, and we are obliged to use and manage these resources wisely in serving the Lord. God's idea was not to have a world composed exclusively of primitive areas. Before the Fall (Gen. 2:15) Adam was to cultivate and keep the Garden of Eden. After the Fall the same command pertains to the application of technology to this fallen world, a world that "groans" in travail (Rom. 8:22). Technology can benefit mankind in exercising proper dominion, and thus remove some of the effects of the Fall (such as curing disease, breeding livestock, or growing better crops).

Technology is neither good nor evil. The worldview behind the particular technology determines its value. In the Old Testament, technology was used both for good (e.g., the building of the ark, Gen. 6) and for evil (e.g., the building of the Tower of Babel, Gen. 11). Therefore, the focus should not be so much on the technology itself as on the philosophical motivation behind its use. Here are three important principles that should be considered.

First, technology should be seen as a tool, not as an end in itself. There is nothing sacred about technology. Unfortunately, Western culture tends to rely on it more than is appropriate. If a computer, for example, proves a particular point, people have a greater tendency to believe it than if the answer was a well-reasoned conclusion given by a person. If a machine can do the job, employers are prone to mechanize, even if human labor does a better or more creative job. Often our society unconsciously places machines over man. Humans become servants to machines rather than the other way around.

There is a tendency to look to science and engineering to solve problems that really may be due to human sinfulness (wars, prejudice, greed), the fallenness of the world (death, disease), or God's curse on Adam (finite resources). In Western culture especially, we tend to believe that technology will save us from our problems, and thus we use technology as a substitute for God. Christians must not fall into this trap but instead, must exhibit their ultimate dependence on God. Christians must also differentiate between problems that demand a technological solution and ones that can be remedied by a social or spiritual one.

Second, technology should be applied in different ways, according to specific instructions. For example, there are distinctions between man and animal that, because we are created in God's image (Gen. 1:26-27), call for different applications of medical science. Using artificial insemination to improve the genetic fitness of livestock does not justify using it on human beings. Christians should resist the idea that just because we *can* do something, we *should* do it. Technological ability does not grant moral permission.

Third, ethics, rather than technology, must determine the direction of our society. Jacques Ellul has expressed the concern that technology moves society instead of vice versa.[1] Our society today seems all too motivated by a technological imperative in our culture. The technological ability to do something is not the same as a moral imperative to do it. Technology should not determine ethics.

Although scientists might possess the technological ability to be gods, they nevertheless lack the capacity to act like gods. Too often, man has tried to use technology

---

[1] Jacques Ellul, *The Technological Society* (New York: Vintage, 1964).

to become God. He uses it to work out his own physical salvation, to enhance his own development, or even to attempt to create life. Christians who take seriously human fallenness will humbly admit that we often do not know enough about God's creation to use technology wisely. The reality of human sinfulness means that society should be careful to prevent the use of technology for greed and exploitation.

Technology's fruits can be both sweet and bitter. C. S. Lewis writes in the *Abolition of Man*, "From this point of view, what we call Man's power over Nature turns out to be power exercised by some men over men with Nature as its instrument. . . . There neither is nor can be any simple increase of power on Man's side. Each new power won *by* man is a power *over* man as well. Each advance leaves him weaker as well as stronger. In every victory, besides being the general who triumphs, he is also the prisoner who follows the triumphal car."[2]

Christians must bring strong biblical critique to each technological advance and analyze its impact. The goal should be to liberate the positive effects of technology while restraining negative effects by setting up appropriate constraints against abuse.

The Challenge of Biotechnology

The age of biotechnology has arrived. For the first time in human history, it is possible to completely redesign existing organisms, including man, and to direct the genetic and reproductive constitution of every living thing. Scientists are no longer limited to breeding and cross-pollination. Powerful genetic tools allow us to change genetic structure at the microscopic level and bypass the normal processes of reproduction.

---

[2] C. S. Lewis, *The Abolition of Man* (New York: Macmillan, 1947), 6869, 71 (italics his).

For the first time in human history, it is also possible to make multiple copies of any existing organism or of certain sections of its genetic structure. This ability to clone existing organisms or their genes gives scientists a powerful tool to reproduce helpful and useful genetic material within a population.

Scientists are also developing techniques to treat and cure genetic diseases through genetic surgery and genetic therapy. They can already identify genetic sequences that are defective, and soon scientists will be able to replace these defects with properly functioning genes.

Gene splicing (known as recombinant DNA technology) is fundamentally different from other forms of genetic breeding used in the past. Breeding programs work on existing arrays of genetic variability in a species, isolating specific genetic traits through selective breeding. Scientists using gene splicing can essentially "stack" the deck or even produce an entirely new deck of genetic "cards."

However, this powerful ability to change the genetic deck of cards also raises substantial scientific concerns that some "sleight-of-hand" would produce dangerous consequences. Ethan Singer said, "Those who are powerful in society will do the shuffling; their genes will be shuffled in one direction, while the genes of the rest of us will get shuffled in another."[3] Also, there is the concern that a reshuffled deck of genes might create an Andromeda strain similar to the one envisioned by Michael Crichton is his book by the same title.[4] A microorganism might inadvertently be given the genetic structure for some pathogen for which, there is no antidote or vaccine.

---

[3] Ethan Singer, cited in Nicholas Wade, "Gene Splicing: Congress Starts Framing Law for Research," *Science*, 1 April 1977, 39.

[4] Michael Crichton, *The Andromeda Strain* (New York: Dell, 1969).

The potential benefits of gene splicing are significant. First, the technology can be used to produce medically important substances. The list of these substances is quite large and would include insulin, interferon, and human growth hormone. The technology also has great application in the field of immunology. In order to protect organisms from viral disease, doctors must inject a killed or attenuated virus. Scientists can use the technology to disable a toxin gene, thus producing a viral substance that triggers production of antibodies without the possibility of producing the disease.

A second benefit is in the field of agriculture. This technology can improve the genetic fitness of various plant species. Basic research using this technology could increase the efficiency of photosynthesis, increase plant resistance (to salinity, to drought, to viruses), and reduce a plant's demand for nitrogen fertilizer.

Third, gene splicing can aid industrial and environmental processes. Industries that manufacture drugs, plastics, industrial chemicals, vitamins, and cheese will benefit from this technology. Also, scientists have begun to develop organisms that can clean up oil spills or toxic wastes.

This last benefit, however, also raises one of the greatest scientific concerns over the use of biotechnology. The escape (or even intentional release) of a genetically engineered organism might wreak havoc on the environment. Scientists have created microorganisms that dissolve oil spills or reduce frost on plants. Critics of gene splicing fear that radically altered organisms could occupy new ecological niches, destroy existing ecosystems, or drive certain species to extinction.

A significant question is whether life should be patented at all. Most religious leaders say no. A 1995 gathering of religious leaders representing virtually every major religious tradition spoke out against the patenting of genetically engineered substances. They argued that life is the creation of God, not humans, and should not be patented as human inventions.[5]

The broader theological question is *whether* genetic engineering should be used and, if permitted, *how* it should be used. The natural reaction for many in society is to reject new forms of technology because they are dangerous. Christians, however, should take into account God's command to humankind in the cultural mandate (Gen. 1:28). Christians should avoid the reflex reaction that scientists should not tinker with life; instead, Christians should consider how this technology should be used responsibly.

One key issue is the worldview behind most scientific research. Modern science rests on an evolutionary assumption. Many scientists assume that life on this planet is the result of millions of years of a chance evolutionary process. Therefore they conclude that intelligent scientists can do a better job of directing the evolutionary process than nature can do by chance. Even evolutionary scientists warn of this potential danger. Ethan Singer believes that scientists will "verify a few predictions, and then gradually forget that knowing something isn't the same as knowing everything . . . At each stage we will get a little cockier, a little surer we know all the possibilities."[6]

In essence, biotechnology gives scientists the tools they have always wanted to drive the evolutionary spiral higher and higher. Julian Huxley looked forward to the day in which scientists could fill the "position of business

---

[5] Kenneth Woodward, "Thou Shalt Not Patent!" *Newsweek*, 29 May 1995, 68.

[6] Testimony by Ethan Singer before the Subcommittee on Health and the Environment, House Committee on Interstate and Foreign Commerce, *Hearings*, 15 March 1977, 79.

manager for the cosmic process of evolution."[7] Certainly, this technology enables scientists to create new forms of life and alter existing forms in ways that have been impossible until now.

How should Christians respond? They should humbly acknowledge that God is the sovereign Creator and that man has finite knowledge. Genetic engineering gives scientists the technological ability to be gods, but they lack the wisdom, knowledge, and moral capacity to act like God.

Even evolutionary scientists who deny the existence of God and believe that all life is the result of an impersonal evolutionary process express concern about the potential dangers of this technology. Erwin Chargaff asked, "Have we the right to counteract, irreversibly, the evolutionary wisdom of millions of years, in order to satisfy the ambition and curiosity of a few scientists?"[8] His answer is no. The Christian's answer should also be the same when we realize that God is the Creator of life. We do not have the right to "rewrite the fifth day of creation."[9]

What is the place for genetic engineering within a biblical framework? The answer to that question can be found by distinguishing between two types of research. The first could be called genetic repair. This research attempts to remove genetic defects and develop techniques that will provide treatments for existing diseases. Applications would include various forms of genetic therapy and genetic surgery as well as

---

[7] Julian Huxley, cited in Joseph Fletcher, *The Ethics of Genetic Control* (Garden City, NY: Anchor, 1974), 8.

[8] Erwin Chargaff, cited in George Wald, "The Case against Genetic Engineering," *The Sciences*, May 1976, 10.

[9] Nancy McCann, "The DNA Maelstrom: Science and Industry Rewrite the Fifth Day of Creation," *Sojourners*, May 1977, 2326.

modifications of existing microorganisms to produce beneficial results.

The Human Genome Project has been able to pinpoint the location and sequence of the approximately 100,000 human genes. Further advances in biotechnology will allow scientists to repair these defective sequences and eventually remove these genetic diseases from our population.

Genetic disease is not part of God's plan for the world. It is the result of the Fall (Gen. 3). Christians can apply technology to fight these evils without being accused of fighting against God's will. Genetic engineering can and should be used to treat and cure genetic diseases.

A second type of research is the creation of new forms of life. While minor modifications of existing organisms may be permissible, Christians should be concerned about the large-scale production of novel life forms. That potential impact on the environment and on mankind could be considerable. Science is replete with examples of what can happen when an existing organism is introduced into a new environment (e.g., the rabbit into Australia, the rat to Hawaii, or the gypsy moth in the United States). One can only imagine the potential devastation that could occur when a newly created organism is introduced into a new environment.

God created plants and animals as "kinds" (Gen. 1:24). While there is minor variability within these created kinds, there are built-in barriers between these created kinds. Redesigning creatures of any kind cannot be predicted the same way new elements on the periodic chart can be predicted for properties even before they are discovered. Recombinant DNA technology offers great promise in treating genetic disease, but Christians should also be vigilant. While this technology should be used to repair genetic defects, it should not be used to confer the role of creator on scientists.

A related issue in the field of biotechnology is human cloning. It appears that the cloning of a human being will no doubt take place sometime in the future since many other mammals have been cloned. Proponents of human cloning argue that it would be a worthwhile scientific endeavor for at least three reasons. First, cloning could be used to produce spare parts. The clone would be genetically identical to the original person so that a donated organ would not be rejected by the immune system. Second, they argue that cloning might be a way to replace a lost child. A dying infant or child could be cloned so that a couple would replace the child with a genetically identical child.

While cloning of various organisms may be permissible, cloning a human being raises significant questions beginning with the issue of the sanctity of life. Human beings are created in the image of God (Gen. 1:27-28) and therefore differ from animals. Human cloning would certainly threaten the sanctity of human life at a number of levels. First, cloning is an inefficient process of procreation as shown in cloning of a sheep. Second, cloning would no doubt produce genetic accidents. Previous experiments with frogs produced numerous embryos that did not survive, and many of those that did survive developed into grotesque monsters. Third, researchers often clone human embryos for various experiments. Although the National Bioethics Advisory Commission did ban cloning of human beings, it permitted the cloning of human embryos for research. Since these embryos are ultimately destroyed, this research raises the same pro-life concerns discussed in the chapter on abortion.

Cloning represents a tampering with the reproductive process at the most basic level. Cloning a human being certainly strays substantially from God's intended procedure of a man and woman producing children within the bounds of matrimony (Gen. 2:24). All sorts of bizarre scenarios can be envisioned. Some homosexual advocates argue that cloning would be an ideal way for homosexual men to reproduce themselves.

Although this would be an alternative form of reproduction, it is reasonable to believe that human clones would still be fully human. For example, some people wonder if a clone would have a soul since this would be such a diversion from God's intended process of procreation. A traducian view of the origin of the soul, where a person receives both body and soul from his parents rather than an act of special creation by God, would imply that a cloned human being would have a soul. In a sense, a clone would be no different from an identical twin.

Human cloning, like other forms of genetic engineering, could be used to usher in a "brave new world." James Bonner says "there is nothing to prevent us from taking a thousand [cells]. We could grow any desired number of genetically identical people from individuals who have desirable characteristics."[10] Such a vision conjures up images of Alphas, Betas, Gammas, and Deltas from Aldous Huxley's book *Brave New World* and provides a dismal contrast to God's creation of each individual as unique.

Each person contributes to both the unity and diversity of humanity. This is perhaps best expressed by the Jewish Midrash: "For a man stamps many coins in one mold and they are all alike; but the King who is king over all kings, the Holy One blessed be he, stamped every man in the mold of the first man, yet not one of

---

[10] James Bonner, quoted in *Los Angeles Times*, 17 May 1971, 1.

them resembles his fellow."[11] Christians should reject future research plans to clone a human being and should reject using cloning as an alternative means of reproduction.

The Challenge of Information Technology

The information revolution is the latest technological advance Christians must consider. The shift to computers and an information-based society has been swift as well as spectacular. The first electronic digital computer, ENIAC, weighed thirty tons, had 18,000 vacuum tubes, and occupied a space as large as a boxcar.[12] Less than forty years later, many hand-held calculators had comparable computing power for a few dollars. Today most people have a computer on their desk with more computing power than engineers could imagine just a few years ago.

The impact of computers on our society was probably best seen when in 1982 *Time* magazine picked the computer as its "Man of the Year"—actually listing it as "Machine of the Year. It is hard to imagine a picture of the Spirit of St. Louis or an Apollo lander on the magazine cover under a banner "Machine of the Year." This perhaps shows how influential the computer has become in our society.

The computer has become helpful in managing knowledge at a time when the amount of information is expanding exponentially. Buckminster Fuller created the 'Knowledge Doubling Curve'; he noticed that until 1900 human knowledge doubled approximately every century.

---

[11] N. N. Glazer, *Hammer on the Rock: A Short Midrash Reader* (New York: Schocken, 1962), 15.

[12] Philip Elmer-De-Witt, "A Birthday Party for ENIAC," *Time*, 24 February 1986, 63.

Now it is doubling every 12 months.[13] In a sense the computer age and the information, age seems to go hand in hand.

The rapid development and deployment of computing power, however, has also raised some significant social and moral questions. People in this society need to think clearly about these issues, but often ignore them or become confused.

One key issue is computer crime. In a sense computer, fraud is merely a new field with old problems. Computer crimes are often nothing more than fraud, larceny, and embezzlement carried out by more sophisticated means. The crimes usually involve changing address, records, or files. In short, they are old-fashioned crimes using high technology.

Another concern arises from the centralization of information. Governmental agencies, banks, and businesses use computers to collect information on its citizens and customers. For example, it is estimated that the federal government has on average about fifteen files on each American.[14] Nothing is inherently wrong with collecting information if the information can be kept confidential and is not used for immoral actions. Unfortunately, this is often difficult to guarantee.

In an information-based society, the centralization of information can be as dangerous as the centralization of power. Given that sinful man in a fallen world, we should be concerned about the collection and manipulation of vast amounts of personal information.

---

[13] Patrice Lewis, "Is Knowledge doubling?" *WorldNetDaily*, 27 May 2016,

http://www.wnd.com/2016/05/is-knowledge-doubling-or-halving/.

[14] Ted Gest, "Who Is Watching You?" *U.S. News and World Report*, 12 July 1982, 35.

In the past, centralized information processing was used for persecution. When Adolf Hitler's Gestapo began rounding up millions of Jews, information about their religious affiliation was stored in shoeboxes. U.S. Census Bureau punch cards were used to round up Japanese-Americans living on the West Coast at the beginning of World War II.[15] Modern technology makes this task much easier. Governmental agencies routinely collect information about citizens' ethnic origin, race, religion, gross income, and even political preference.

Moreover, the problem it not limited to governmental agencies. Many banking systems, for example, utilize electronic funds-transfer systems. Plans to link these systems together into a national system could also provide a means of tracking the actions of citizens. A centralized banking network could fulfill nearly every information need a malevolent dictator might have. This is not to say that such a thing will happen. It does mean, however, that societies that want to monitor their citizens will be able to do so more efficiently with computer technology.

A related problem arises from the confidentiality of computer records. Computer records can be abused like any other system. Reputations built up over a lifetime can be ruined by computer errors and often there is little recourse for the victim. Congress passed the 1974 Privacy Act which allows citizens to find out what records federal bureaucracies have on them and to correct any error. More legislation is needed than this particular act.

The proliferation of computers has presented another set of social and moral concerns. In the recent past, most of that information was centralized and required the expertise of the "high priests of FORTRAN"

---

[15] David Burnham, *The Rise of the Computer State* (New York: Random House, 1983).

to utilize it. Now most people have access to information because of increasing numbers of personal computers and increased access to information through the Internet. This access to information will have many interesting sociological ramifications, and it is also creating a set of troubling ethical questions. The proliferation of computers that can tie into other computers provides more opportunities for computerized crime.

The news media frequently carry reports about computer "hackers" who have been able to gain access to confidential computer systems and obtain or interfere with the data banks. Although these were supposed to be secure systems, enterprising computer hackers broke in anyway. In many cases, this merely involved curious teenagers.

Nevertheless, computer hacking has become a developing area of crime. Criminals might use computer access to forge documents, change records, and draft checks. They can even use computers for blackmail by holding files for ransom and threatening to destroy them if their demands are not met. Unless better methods of security are found, professional criminals will begin to crack computer security codes and gain quick access into sensitive files.

As with most technological breakthroughs, engineers have outrun lawmakers. Computer deployment has created a number of legal questions. First, there is the problem of establishing penalties for cyber crime. Typically, intellectual property has a different status in our criminal justice system. Legal scholars should evaluate the notion that ideas and information need not be protected in the same way as property. Legislators need to enact computer information protection laws that will deter criminals, or even curious computer hackers, from breaking into confidential records.

A second legal problem arises from the question of jurisdiction. Telecommunications allows information to be shared across state and even national borders. Few federal statutes govern this area, and less than half the states have laws dealing with information abuse.

Enforcement will also be a problem for several reasons. One reason is the previously stated problem of jurisdiction. Another is that police departments rarely train their personnel in computer abuse and fraud. A third reason is a lack of personnel. Computers are nearly as ubiquitous as telephones or photocopiers.

Computer fraud also raises questions about the role of insurance companies. How do companies insure an electronic asset? What value does computer information have? These questions also need to be addressed in the future.

Technology and Human Nature

These new technologies will also challenge our views of human nature. Already medical technology is challenging our views of what it means to be human. A key question in the abortion debate is, When does human life begin? Is an embryo human? What about a developing fetus? Although the Bible provides answers to these questions, society often takes its cue from pronouncements that do not square with biblical truth.

Biotechnology raises yet another set of questions. Is a frozen embryo human and deserving of a right to life? Is a clone human? Would a clone have a soul? These and many more questions will have to be answered. Although the Bible doesn't directly address such issues as genetically engineered humans or clones, key biblical passages (Ps. 139, Ps. 51:5) certainly seem to teach that an embryo is a human created in the image of God.

Information technology also raises questions about human nature in an unexpected way. Researchers believe that as computer technology advances, we will begin to analyze the human mind in physical terms. In *The Society of Mind*, Marvin Minsky, a professor at the Massachusetts Institute of Technology, says that "the mind, the soul, the self, are not a singly ghostly entity but a society of agents, deeply integrated, yet each one rather mindless on its own."[16] He dreams of being able to ultimately reduce mind (and therefore human nature) to natural mechanism. Obviously, this is not an empirical statement, but a metaphysical one that attempts to reduce everything (including mind) to matter.

Will we someday elevate computers to the level of humanity? One article asked the question, Would an Intelligent Computer Have a "Right to Life?"[17] Granting computer rights might be something society might consider since many are already willing to grant certain rights to animals.

In a sense, the question is whether an intelligent computer would have a soul and therefore access to fundamental human rights. As bizarre as the question may sound, it was no doubt inevitable. When 17th-century philosopher Gottfried Wilhelm von Leibniz first described a thinking machine, he was careful to point out that this machine would not have a soul—fearful perhaps of reaction from the church.[18] Already scientists predict that computer intelligence will create "an intelligence

---

[16] Richard Lipkin, "Making Machines in Mind's Image," *Insight*, 15 February 1988, 812.

[17] Robert Mueller and Erik Mueller, "Would an Intelligent Computer Have a 'Right to Life?'" *Creative Computing*, August 1983, 14961.

[18] Danny Hillis, "Can They Feel Your Pain?" *Newsweek*, 5 May 1997, 57.

beyond man's" and provide wonderful new capabilities.[19] One of the great challenges in the future will be how to manage new computing power that will outstrip human intelligence.

Once again, this is a challenge for Christians in the 21st century. Human beings are more than just proteins and nucleic acids. Human being are more than bits and bytes. We are created in the image of God and therefore have a spiritual dimension. Perhaps this must be our central message to a world enamored with technology: human beings are created in the image of God and must be treated with dignity and respect.

---

[19] Robert Jastrow, "Toward an Intelligence beyond Man's," *Time*, 20 February 1978, 59.

CHAPTER 2 The Challenge of Transhumanism

Technology can be used for both good and bad purposes. We need to look at the philosophy and worldview behind the use of technology. That is why many Christians have begun to write and speak about the philosophy known as transhumanism.

What exactly is transhumanism? It is an intellectual and cultural movement that seeks to transform the human condition. The leaders of this movement want to use the developing technologies to eliminate aging and enhance human potential (physical, psychological, and mental). Two primary ways they want to do this is through genetic engineering and artificial intelligence. They want to genetically create "the new man," and they want to use technology to turn us into "cyborgs" (which is short for cybernetic organism).

The genetic part of this equation claims that we can use gene splicing and other genetic modification techniques so that genes can be easily transferred between species. This might even create a global super-organism. Christians can certainly endorse the use of genetics to rid humankind of genetic diseases.[20] But we should be concerned about geneticists that want to create a superhuman race. Leon Kass warned that: "Engineering the engineer seems to differ in kind from engineering the engine."[21]

The other part of the equation concerns technology. The leaders of transhumanism believe we are on the cusp of a technological threshold in both artificial intelligence

---

[20] Anderson, Kerby. *Genetic Engineering*. Zondervan, 1982, 96.
[21] Kass, Leon. "The New Biology: What Price Relieving Man's Estate?" *Science*, 19 November 1971, 779.

and human-machine technology. They call the point when humans and machines merge into one as "the Singularity."

Transhumanism in the Movies

Science fiction writers often portray concepts found in transhumanism, but also show the inherent problems with these ideas. Genetic engineering and breeding the human race sounds like a good idea until you watch the movie, "Gattaca."[22] In that future, eugenics plays a key role in determining a person's social class.

Vincent is born without the aid of this technology and is seen as inferior to his brother Anton who was conceived with the aid of genetic selection. Vincent dreams of a career in space, but is constantly reminded of his genetic inferiority and faces discrimination. He decides to impersonate someone with a superior genetic profile. He is accepted into the space program, not on the basis of his ability. The entire interview process is a DNA test. The movie reminds us that there is likely to be significant discrimination of people who are produced "the old fashioned way" in a society that produces children "the new and improved way."

The idea of living in a perfect body that does not age sounds exciting, until you watch the movie, "In Time."[23] A genetic advancement now allows humanity to stop aging at 24, but also requires people to earn more time or die. "Living time" can be transferred between people and essentially has replaced money. But when the clock reaches zero, you die.

Society in the movie is divided into social classes who live in specialized towns called "Time Zones." The

---

[22] Gattaca, http://www.imdb.com/title/tt0119177/

[23] In Time, http://www.imdb.com/title/tt1637688/

poor live in the ghettos and must work hard just to survive and add enough time to their bodies. Meanwhile the rich live in luxury and have all the time they need (and can even live for centuries). Will Salas begins to discover the inequity of the way time in allocated and ultimately upsets the entire social stratification in the "Time Zones." The movie reminds us that living forever may sound inviting, but you eventually wear out. As one rich person says, "your mind is worn out, even though your body may not be. We want, we need, to die."

In the movie "Elyisum," two classes of people exist.[24] Wealthy people live on a luxurious space station called Elysium. They enjoy the best of technology, including medical devices (called Med-Bays) that rid them of disease and injury. The poor live on an overpopulated, devastated Earth and are policed by unemotional and compassionless robots.

Max Da Costa lives in the ruins of Los Angeles and works on an assembly line for a military company that supplies arms and weapons for Elysium. He has an accident at his work and is exposed to lethal radiation. Knowing he only has a few days to live, he works to find a way to get to Elysium and be saved by using on of the Med-Bays. He is able to download a program to his brain that can override the central computer in Elysium. He makes his way to Elysium but dies in the process of uploading the computer program that registers every resident of Earth as a citizen of Elysium. Shuttles are then deployed to take the sick from Earth to Elysium.

What about the idea that technology could allow us to live their lives through humanoid robots in the world while we are safe and protected at home? That may seem appealing until we watch the movie, "Surrogates."[25]

---

[24] Elysium, http://www.imdb.com/title/tt1535108/

[25] Surrogates, http://www.imdb.com/title/tt0986263/

People in the film live through high-tech surrogates who are beautiful, athletic, and remotely controlled. People experience life vicariously from the comfort of their homes.

Agent Tom Green ventures out into the real world to investigate a murder of two people who died when their surrogates were destroyed. That is not supposed to happen. People using a surrogate are protected from harm and pain. They are not supposed to die even if the surrogated is damaged or destroyed. This movie challenges that idea that we should use technology to keep us from living in the real world.

And we can think of many movies that warn us of what might happen in a world where machines control the world. The "Terminator" movie series and the "Matrix" movie series are examples. They remind us that machines should be our servants, not our masters.

Biblical Perspective

How should Christians respond to transhumanism? We should begin by looking at the philosophical foundation of this movement. It begins with the belief that there is no God and we are responsible for our own destiny. It also is based upon an evolutionary foundation that assumes that we are the product of millions of years of chance process.

Therefore, the leaders of transhumanism see genetic engineering as a tool to be used to speed up the process of evolution. We can use genetics to enhance and improve the human race. If we believe that humans are merely the product of the undirected force of evolution, then certainly intelligent scientists can "improve on nature." Julian Huxley looked forward to the day in which scientists could fill the "position of business manager for the cosmic process of evolution."[26]

But if humans are created in the image of God (Genesis 1:27), then we can and should use genetic technology to treat and cure the physical effects of the Fall (Genesis 3). That does not mean we should usurp the role of the Creator and breed a super human race.

The leaders of transhumanism believe we should use technology to improve the human race so that we are perfect and immortal. In many ways, this technological imperative harkens back to the Tower of Babel (Genesis 11). Instead, we should use technology wisely as we exercise dominion over the world (Genesis 1:28).

---

[26] Julian Huxley quoted in Joseph Fletcher's book, *The Ethics of Genetic Control* (Anchor, 1974), 8.

CHAPTER 3 Globalization and the Internet

More than three billion people use the Internet and benefit from the vast amount of information that is available to anyone who connects. But any assessment of the Internet will show that it has provided both surprising virtues and unavoidable vices.

Contrary to the oft-repeated joke, Al Gore did not invent the Internet. It was the creation of the Department of Defense that built it in case of a nuclear attack, but its primary use has been during peace.

The Internet has certainly changed lives. Thomas Friedman in his book, *The World is Flat*, talks about some of the changes.[27] For example, we used to go to the post office to send mail; now most of us also send digitized mail over the Internet known as e-mail. We used to go to bookstores to browse and buy books; now we also browse digitally. We used to buy a CD to listen to music; now many of us obtain our digitized music off the Internet and download it to an MP3 player.

He talks about how the Internet has been the great equalizer. A good example of that is Google. Whether you are a university professor with a high-speed Internet connection or a poor kid in Asia with access to an Internet café, you have the same basic access to research information. The Internet puts an enormous amount of information at our fingertips. Essentially, all of the information on the Internet is available to anyone, anywhere, at any time.

The Internet (and the accompanying digital tools developed to use it) has even changed our language. In

---

[27] Thomas Friedman, *The World is Flat: A Brief History of the Twenty-First Century* (New York: Farrar, Straus and Giroux, 2005).

the past, if you left a message asking when your friend was going to arrive at the airport, usually you would receive a complete sentence. Today the message would be something like AA 635 @ 7:42 PM DFW. Tell a joke in a social media platform like Twitter, and you will receive responses like LOL ("laughing out loud") or ROFL ("rolling on the floor laughing"). As people leave the chat room, they may type BBL ("be back later"). Such abbreviations and computer language are a relatively new phenomenon and were spawned by the growth of the Internet.

I want to take a look at some of the challenges of the Internet as well as the attempt by the government to control aspects of it. While the Internet has certainly provided information to anyone, anywhere, at any time, there are still limits to what the Internet can do in the global world.

Challenge of the Internet

The Internet has provided an opportunity to all of us to have an enormous amount of information at our fingertips. It is truly a wonderful development for those of us who are privileged to live in the 21st century.

But the information superhighway also has some dark back alleys. At the top of the list is pornography. The Internet has made the distribution of pornography much easier. It used to be that someone wanting to view this material had to leave their home and go to the other side of town. The Internet has become the ultimate brown wrapper. Hard core images that used to be difficult to obtain are now only a mouse click away.

Children see pornography at a much younger age than just a decade ago. Sometimes this exposure is intentional; usually, it is accidental. Schools, libraries, and homes using filters often are one step behind those trying to expose more and more people to pornography.

The influence of the Internet on pornography is only one part of a larger story. In my writing on personal and social ethics, I have found that the Internet has made existing social problems worse. When I wrote my book *Moral Dilemmas* back in 1998, I dealt with such problems as drugs, gambling, and pornography. Seven years later when I was writing my new book, *Christian Ethics in Plain Language*, I noticed that every moral issue I discussed was made worse by the Internet. Now my chapter on pornography has a section on cyberporn. My chapter on gambling has a section dealing with online gambling. My chapter on adultery also deals with online affairs.

Internet Regulation

All of these concerns lead to the obvious question. Who will regulate the Internet? In the early day of the Internet, proponents saw it as the cyber-frontier that would be self-regulating. The Internet was to liberate us forever from government, borders, and even our physical selves.

For a time, the self-government of the Internet worked fairly well. Internet pioneers were even successful in fighting off the Communications Decency Act that punished the transmission of "indecent" sexual communications or images on the Internet.[28] But soon national governments began to exercise their authority.

---

[28] Communications Decency Act of 1996, Pub. L. No. 104-104, ti.t. v, 110 Stat. 56, 133-143.

Jack Goldsmith and Tim Wu, in their book, describe the various ways foreign governments have exercised their authority:[29]

• France requires Yahoo to block Internet surfers from France so they cannot purchase Nazi memorabilia.

• The People's Republic of China requires Yahoo to filter materials that might be harmful or threatening to Party rule. Yahoo is essentially an Internet censor for the Communist party.

• The Chinese version of Google is much slower than the American version because the company cooperates with the Chinese government by blocking search words the Party finds offensive (words like Tibet or democracy).

Even more disturbing is the revelation that Yahoo provided information to the Chinese government that led to the imprisonment of Chinese journalists and pro-democracy leaders. Reporters Without Borders found that Yahoo has been implicated in most of the people they were defending.

Columnist Clarence Page points out that: "Microsoft cooperates in censoring or deleting blogs that offend the Chinese government's sensibilities. Cisco provides the hardware that gives China the best Internet-blocking and user-tracking technology on the planet."[30]

All of this censorship and cooperation with foreign governments is disturbing, but it also underscores an important point. For years, proponents of the Internet have argued that we can't (or shouldn't) block Internet

---

[29] Jack Goldsmith and Tim Wu, *Who Controls the Internet?* (NY: Oxford University Press, 2006).

[30] Clarence Page, "Google caves to China's censors," *Chicago Tribune*, 16 Apr. 2006, . www.chicagotribune.com/news/columnists/chi-0604160321apr16,0,4616158.column

pornography or that we can't regulate what pedophiles do on the Internet. These recent revelations about Yahoo, Google, and Microsoft show that they can and do block information.

Government and Intermediaries

Governments have been able to exercise control over the Internet in various ways. This should not be too surprising. The book *Who Controls the Internet?* points out that while some stores in New York's Chinatown sell counterfeit Gucci bags and Rolex watches, you don't find these same products in local stores. That is because the "most important targets of the laws against counterfeits—trademark laws—are local retailers."[31]

The U.S. government might not be able to go after manufacturers in China or Thailand that produce these counterfeits, but they certainly can go after retail stores. That's why you won't find these counterfeit goods in a Wal-Mart store. And while it is true that by controlling Wal-Mart or Sears doesn't eliminate counterfeit goods, government still can adequately control the flow of these goods by focusing on these intermediaries.

Governments often control behavior through intermediaries. "Pharmacists and doctors are made into gatekeepers charged with preventing certain forms of drug abuse. Bartenders are responsible for preventing their customers from driving drunk."[32]

As the Internet has grown, there has also been an increase in new intermediaries. These would include Internet Service Providers (ISPs), search engines, browsers, etc. In a sense, the Internet has made the network itself the intermediary. And this has made it possible for

---
[31] Goldsmith and Wu, Who Controls the Internet?, 68.
[32] Ibid., 68.

governments to exert their control over the Internet. "Sometimes the government-controlled intermediary is Wal-Mart preventing consumer access to counterfeit products, sometimes it is the bartender enforcing drinking age laws, and sometimes it is an ISP blocking access to illegal information."[33]

More than a decade ago, the German government raided the Bavarian offices of Compuserve because they failed to prevent the distribution of child pornography even though it originated outside of Germany.[34] In 2001, the British government threatened certain sites with criminal prosecution for distributing illegal adoption sites. The British ISPs agreed to block the sites so that British citizens could not access them.[35]

Internet Service Providers, therefore, are the obvious target for governmental control. In a sense, they are the most important gatekeepers to the Internet.[36]

Governmental control over the Internet is not perfect nor is it complete. But the control over intermediaries has allowed territorial governments to exercise much great control and regulation of the Internet than many of the pioneers of cyberspace would have imagined.

Globalization and Government

Globalization and technology (including the Internet) have made it much easier to move information

---

[33] Ibid., 72.

[34] Edmund L. Andrews, "Germany Charges Compuserve Manager," *New York Times*, 17 Apr. 1997.

[35] John Carvel, "Prison Terms for Illegal Adoptions: Internet Babies Case Prompts Tough New Sanctions," *Guardian* (UK), 15 March 2001.

[36] Jonathan Zittrain, "Internet Points of Control," 44 B.C.L. Rev. 653, 664-69 (2003).

around the world. There is no doubt that the Internet has accelerated the speed of transmission and thus made the world smaller. It is much easier for people around the world to access information and share it with others in this global information infrastructure.

Those who address the issue of globalization also believe that it diminishes the relevance of borders, territorial governments, and geography. Thomas Friedman believes that the Internet and other technologies are flattening the world "without regard to geography, distance, or, in the near future, even language."[37]

In one sense, this is true. The lower costs of moving information and the sheer amount of information exchanged on the Internet have made it more difficult for governments to suppress information they do not like. The explosive growth of blogs and web pages have provided a necessary outlet for opinion and information.

It is also true that there has been some self-governing behavior on the Internet. Friedman, for example, describes eBay as a "self-governing nation-state—the V.R.e., the Virtual Republic of eBay." The CEO of eBay even says, "People will say that eBay restored my faith in humanity—contrary to a world where people are cheating and don't give people the benefit of the doubt."[38]

However, it also true that territorial governments work with eBay to arrest and prosecute those who are cheaters or who use the website in illegal ways. And it also relies on a banking system and the potential of governmental prosecution of fraud.

---

[37] Thomas Friedman, *The World is Flat*, 176.

[38] Ibid., 455.

We have also seen in this article that governments have also been able to exert their influence and authority over the Internet. They have been able to use the political process to alter or block information coming into their country and have been able to shape the Internet in ways that the early pioneers of the Internet did not foresee.

Goldsmith and Wu believe that those talking about the force of globalization often naively believe that countries will be powerless in the face of globalization and the Internet. "When globalization enthusiasts miss these points, it is usually because they are in the grips of a strange technological determinism that views the Internet as an unstoppable juggernaut that will overrun the old and outdated determinants of human organization."[39]

There is still a legitimate function of the government (Romans 13:1-7) even in this new world of cyberspace. Contrary to the perceived assumption that the Internet will shape governments and move us quickly toward globalization, there is good evidence to suggest that governments will in many ways shape the Internet.

---

[39] Goldsmith and Wu, Who Controls the Internet?, 183.

CHAPTER 4 Big Data and Big Brother

We live in a world of "Big Data." But what happens when Big Data meets Big Government? You end up with Big Brother and intrusive surveillance.

Big Data

First, let us define "Big Data." This is a new way people are trying to describe this sea of digital facts, figures, products, books, music, video, and much more. All of this is at our fingertips through computers and smart phones. And there is a lot of data. Eric Schmidt, executive chairman for Google, estimates that humans now create in two days the same amount of data that it took from the dawn of civilization until 2003 to create.[40]

This remarkable change in our world has happened quickly and seamlessly. Today we take for granted that we can create data and access data instantaneously. Pick up the book, *The Human Face of Big Data*, and look at the pictures and stories that describe the powerful impact the tsunami of data is having on our lives and our world.[41] Look at how this vast amount of data is being used by individuals, universities, and companies to answer questions, pull together information, and persuade us to purchase various goods and services.

---

[40] "Eric Schmidt: Every 2 Days We Create As Much Information As We Did Up To 2003," *Tech Crunch*, 4 August 2010, http://techcrunch.com/2010/08/04/schmidt-data/?utm_source=feedburner&utm_medium=feed&utm_campaign=Feed:+Techcrunch+(TechCrunch).

[41] Rick Smolen and Jennifer Erwitt, *The Human Face of Big Data* (Against All Odds Productions, 2012).

One article in *USA Today* explains how "Big Data" will transform our lives and lifestyles.[42] Retailers can target you with online purchasing appeals because of the data they already collect from you when you are online. They can suggest books, videos, and various products you would be interested in based on previous searches or purchases.

If you have a smartphone, think of how you already depend on it in ways that would have been unimaginable a decade ago. It can help answer a question someone poses. It can direct you to a place to eat. If you need gas for your car, it can tell you where the closest gas station is located.

"Big Data" also provides power through instant access to information. Juan Enriquez, author of *As the Future Catches You*, writes: "Today, a street fruit stall in Mumbai can access more information, maps, statistics, academic papers, price trends, futures markets, and data than a U.S. President could only a few decades ago."[43]

Big Data gives us the ability to collect and analyze information in ways never before possible. This gives trend watchers, businesses, corporations, and governments the ability to understand the world in new and more accurate ways.

Another challenge is the enormous amount of data. Nearly a century ago, a dystopian novel imagined a world where every building was made of glass so that various authorities could monitor what citizens are doing every minute of the day. Dan Gardner suggests that the world of Big Data already makes that possible.

---

[42] Chuck Raasch, "Big Data transforms our lives and lifestyles," *USA Today*, 13 December 2012.

[43] Juan Enriquez, "Big Data: You Have No Idea How Much It Will Change Your Life," *INC*, http://www.inc.com/juan-enriquez/big-data-you-have-no-idea-how-much-it-is-changing-your-life.html.

He says we are awash in an ocean of information. "Every time someone clicks on something at Amazon, it's recorded, and another drop is added to the ocean. . . . Every time a customs officer checks a passport, every time someone posts to Facebook, every time someone does a Google search – the ocean swells."[44]

Anyone who has access to that data can begin to use powerful computer algorithms to sift through texts, purchases, posts, photos, and videos to extract more data and trends. Gardner says it will be able to extract meaning and "sort through masses of numbers and find the hidden pattern, the unexpected correlation, the surprising connection. That ability is growing at astonishing speed."

This ocean of "Big Data" can be intrusive. The government, businesses, and even hackers can paint a picture of you that is more accurate than you might want them to know. It is as if we do live in a world where all the buildings are made of glass.

Another concern is what many have called Dark Data. Marc Goodman has written about the phenomenon of Dark Data and is concerned. He has worked on security issues in more than 70 countries and sees the possibilities for criminals in our digital world.[45]

He reminds us that criminals and terrorists have found ways to use these new devices and innovations. Sadly, we often underestimate their creativity and can easily be a step behind those who intend us harm. Sometimes they have better access to information than law enforcement and Homeland Security.

---

[44] Dan Gardner, "Big Data could know us better than we know ourselves," *Ottawa Citizen*, 27 April 2012.

[45] Marc Goodman, "Dark Data," *The Human Face of Big Data*, 74-77.

Drug-runners in Mexico not only have the latest smartphones but have actually been building their own encrypted radio networks in a majority of the states in our country. Drug cartels in Columbia are using their vast wealth from drugs "to fund research and development programs in everything from robotics to supply chain management."

During the terrorist attack in Mumbai five years ago, the terrorists were armed not only "with the standard artillery and explosives, but also with satellite phones, Blackberrys, night vision goggles, and satellite imagery." If that is what terrorists had access to years ago, it is reasonable to assume that the next terrorist attack will come from terrorists using technology that is even more sophisticated.

These new technological advances and the incredible amount of data will no doubt make our world a better place. But we should also realize that criminals and terrorists will also be there to exploit it. We need to do two things. First, train those in law enforcement and counterterrorism in the latest technology. Second, make sure the good guys win the technological arms race against the bad guys.

Big Brother

Big Data matched with Big Government can give us Big Brother. The concept of Big Brother was developed in George Orwell's book, 1984. Big Brother is a fictional character who rules Oceania with total dictatorial control. Everyone in the society is under surveillance by the authorizes through "telescreens." Citizens are constantly reminded that: "Big Brother is watching you."

Surveillance of society is much easier in the 21st century due to cameras, computers, and the efficient analysis of Big Data. Not all of this surveillance is bad. It helps us catch terrorist. For example, the two terrorists who blew up a bomb at the Boston Marathon were caught because of all this new technology. Smartphone pictures identified them. Infrared cameras verified that the brother was in a backyard boat. In fact, the best evidence of their evil actions came from a Lord and Taylor department store security camera.

This is not the first time surveillance technology has helped catch terrorists and evildoers. Cameras in London helped identify the terrorists in 2005. Surveillance video captured the Tucson shootings in 2011. No doubt Big Data and surveillance technology are potent weapons against terrorism.

What about our privacy? Representative Peter King (R-NY) explains: "If you walk down the street, anyone can look at you, anyone can see where you are going. You have no expectation of privacy when you are out in public."[46]

While that may be true, video surveillance is much more intrusive than that. Most of us have been in a shopping mall or a building and needed to adjust our clothing, clean our nose, whatever. We go around the corner thinking we are in private to attend to that need. Then we look up afterward and see a video camera that has recorded everything we just did. Maybe you were doing something silly or embarrassing only to look up and see a crowd of people taking pictures or videos of you with their phones.

Each year we seem to accept more video surveillance at the expense of our civil liberties. Think about it, in airports and government buildings you are always on camera, except perhaps when you are a

---

[46] Yager Jordy, and Herb, Jeremy. "Caught on camera: Boston manhunt sparks debate over more surveillance." *The Hill*, 22 April 2013, http://thehill.com/homenews/house/295183-caught-on-camera.

bathroom stall. With more cameras on street corners, we are approaching a level of video surveillance that reminds us of the movie "The Truman Show."

One television show that reminds us of this surveillance begins with these words: "You are being watched. The government has a secret system: a machine that spies on you every hour of every day. I know because I built it. I designed the machine to detect acts of terror, but it sees everything."

The program is the CBS series, *Person of Interest*. The creator of the program Jonathan Nolan hit a cultural nerve about our increasing lack of privacy. In her article about the program, Susan Karlin reminds us that the storyline is fiction but based on real-life source material that Jonathan Nolan cited in his interview with her. He got some of his ideas from books like *The Watchers: The Rise of America's Surveillance State* and from the government's defunct Total Information Awareness Office.

This is not the first time Jonathan Nolan has raised the question of surveillance in the scripts he has written. When he co-wrote the script for the movie *The Dark Knight*, he inserted a scene where Batman turns all of the Gotham City cell phones into tracking devices so he can find the location of The Joker.

According to Susan Karlin, "Nolan got a taste of encroaching surveillance while growing up in the North London neighborhood of Highgate. 'Scotland Yard began putting cameras up everywhere,' he recalls of a time long before local phone hacking scandals erupted. 'There were cameras out on street corners; English police employed cameras. When I moved to the States at 12, there weren't any cameras. Now you're seeing some cities catching up. In Manhattan, they counted 5,000 in 2005. In 2010, the number was uncountable.'"[47] When you add all the cell phone cameras in the population to these other cameras, you can easily see we have lost our privacy.

We are just beginning to learn the level of surveillance we are under due to the data collection of the National Security Agency[48] (NSA). One story reported that the NSA violated the Constitution over a three-year span when it collected at least 56,000 emails without appropriate privacy protections. We have also learned that the Foreign Intelligence Surveillance Court criticized the NSA for "misrepresenting" its practices.

We have been assured that the NSA only is able to track the origin, destination, and length of a phone call. We have been assured that the NSA isn't listening in to phone calls or reading emails. Then we find out that the NSA has built a surveillance network that is able to read 3 out of every 4 emails sent in the United States.

Many citizens are becoming concerned about this intrusion into our lives. We want the government to catch terrorists and foil potential terrorist attacks. But we also would like the government to respect our privacy. Sadly, this new technology makes it easier than ever to violate our privacy. Most politicians are willing to let the surveillance state grow because they fear the next terrorist attack that will bring the inevitable questions of whether the government did enough.

Will the data NSA is collecting be misused? Columnist Peggy Noonan challenged the three assumptions many people make. "If you assume all the information that can and will be gleaned will be confined to NSA and national security purposes, you are not

---

[47] Karlin, Susan. "Person of Interest Creator Jonathan Nolan Isn't Paranoid—Or Is He? *Fast Company*, 21 September 2011.

[48] Gorman, Siobhan. "Secret Court Faulted NSA for Collecting Domestic Data." *Wall Street Journal*, 21 August, 2013.

sufficiently imaginative or informed. If you believe the information will never be used wrongly or recklessly, you are touchingly innocent. If you assume you can trust the administration on this issue, you are not following the bouncing ball."[49]

Let us look at those three assumptions. First, we know that at least some of the information gleaned by the NSA has been used in other venues. Second, it is likely some will be used wrongly. Given human sinfulness and political ambition, it is likely that more will leak over time and it will be used recklessly. Third, we already know that we cannot trust what the administration has said. We already have had the Director of Intelligence testify that we don't have a domestic surveillance program when clearly we do. We have had the president essentially say the same thing.

Defenders of this level of surveillance point out that the government is merely collecting phone records. They are not wiretapping telephone conversations. That is a critical distinction. The Fourth Amendment does not protect telephone record information. Phone records are very different from the content of telephone conversations. While that is true, we should understand how much information even phone records provide.

If the government has your phone records, it may not know what you said in the phone conversation. But it might have a reasonable guess. If you called the local pizza parlor, the government might not have any idea what type of pizza you ordered. But if you called the local Planned Parenthood on a number of occasions, it could assume you were trying to schedule an abortion. If you called the campaign offices of a candidate, it could

---

[49] Noonan, Peggy. "A Nation of Sullen Paranoids." *Wall Street Journal*, 23 August 2013.

probably guess who you would vote for in the next election.

Of course, you might argue that such information is irrelevant to the government since the goal of such data mining is to search for trends, patterns, associations, and networks of terrorists. In other words, your phone record information wouldn't be made public because it isn't relevant to catching bad guys. Tell that to the National Organization for Marriage that had their confidential IRS information leaked to a liberal group. This example alone illustrates how information could and will be used wrongly and recklessly.

CHAPTER 5 Privacy and Homeland Security

Every day we seem to wake up to news about another terrorist threat, so it's not surprising that Americans are placing more of their faith in the government to protect them. But there are also important questions being raised about our loss of privacy and constitutional protections.

A Supersnoop's Dream

The Department of Homeland Security is a huge bureaucracy. Congress created it by combining twenty-two existing agencies and 170,000 federal employees with an annual budget of approximately $35 billion. While the implications of this megamerger of governmental agencies will be debated for some time, some columnists question the impact it is having on our private lives.

The *Washington Times* called it "A Supersnoop's Dream." Columnist William Safire of the *New York Times* wrote a column entitled "You Are a Suspect" in which he warned of a dangerous intrusion into our lives. He predicted years ago that if the Homeland Security Act were not amended before passage, the following would happen to you:[50]

• Every purchase you make with a credit card, every magazine subscription you buy and medical prescription you fill, every Web site you visit and e-mail you send or receive, every academic grade you receive, every bank deposit you make, every trip you book and every event

---

[50] William Safire, 'You Are a Suspect," *New York Times*, 14 Nov. 2002.

you attend—all these transactions and communications will go into what the Defense Department describes as a virtual, centralized grand database.

• To this computerized dossier on your private life from commercial sources, add every piece of information that government has about you—passport application, driver's license and bridge toll records, judicial and divorce records, complaints from nosy neighbors to the F.B.I., your lifetime paper trail plus the latest hidden camera surveillance—and you have the supersnoop's dream: a Total Information Awareness about every U.S. citizen.

It is important to point out that these concerns about a potential invasion of privacy did not start with the passage of the Homeland Security Act. Over a year ago, critics pointed to the hastily passed U.S.A. Patriot Act, which widened the scope of the Foreign Intelligence Surveillance Act and weakened 15 privacy laws.

On the other hand, there are many who argue that these new powers are necessary to catch terrorists. Cal Thomas, for example, writes that: "Most Americans would probably favor a more aggressive and empowered federal government if it lessens the likelihood of further terrorism. The niceties of civil liberties appear to have been lost on the 9/11 hijackers and countries from which they came. Wartime rules must be different from those in peacetime."[51]

The Patriot Act

Let us look more closely at the U.S.A. Patriot Act. When Senator Russ Feingold voted against the Act, he

---

[51] Cal Thomas, "More Power to the Government," 21 Nov. 2002.

made these comments from the Senate floor on October 11, 2001:[52]

> "There is no doubt that if we lived in a police state, it would be easier to catch terrorists. If we lived in a country where police were allowed to search your home at any time for any reason; if we lived in a country where the government is entitled to open your mail, eavesdrop on your phone conversations, or intercept your e-mail communications; if we lived in a country where people could be held indefinitely based on what they write or think, or based on mere suspicion that they are up to no good, the government would probably discover more terrorists or would-be terrorists, just as it would find more lawbreakers generally. But that wouldn't be a country in which we would want to live."

Most would agree that the Patriot Act weakens grand jury secrecy. Already there is criticism that grand juries have become mere tools of the prosecution and have lost their independence. By destroying its secrecy, any federal official or bureaucrat can "share" grand jury testimony or wiretap information.

The Patriot Act also weakens Fourth Amendment protection against unreasonable searches and seizures. Under the Act, law-enforcement agencies can in "rare instances" search a person's home without informing that homeowner for up to ninety days. This so-called "sneak and peek" provision can be used to sneak into your home, and even implant a hidden "key logger" device on

---

[52] Senator Russ Feingold, remarks about the USA Patriot Act, 25 Oct. 2001.

a suspect's computer (allowing federal officials to capture passwords and monitor every keystroke).

And, the Patriot Act weakens financial privacy. The bill added additional amendments and improvements to the Bank Secrecy Act, which already encourages FDIC member banks to profile account holders and report to the government (FBI, IRS, DEA) when you deviate from your usual spending or deposit habits. The Act exempts bank employees from liability for false reporting of a money laundering violation.

Michael Scardaville of the Heritage Foundation, however, isn't concerned about conferring this new power on bureaucrats. "Even if they wanted to, the program's employees simply won't have time to monitor who plays football pools, who has asthma, who surfs what Web site or even who deals cocaine or steals cars. They'll begin with intelligence reports about people already suspected of terrorism."[53]

Immigration Threats

Lincoln Caplan, writing in the November-December issue of *Legal Affairs* (a magazine of the Yale Law School), said that the U.S.A. Patriot Act "authorized law enforcement agencies to inspect the most personal kinds of information — medical records, bank statements, college transcripts, even church memberships. But what is more startling than the scope of these new powers is that

---

[53] Michael Scardaville, "TIA Targets Terrorists, Not Privacy," 22 Nov. 2002,
http://www.heritage.org/research/commentary/2002/11/tia-targets-terrorists-not-privacy

the government can use them on people who aren't suspected of committing a crime."[54]

Although there has been some concern expressed about the intrusion of government into our lives, an even greater concern is how the Homeland Security Act fails to address the real threat to our country through lax enforcement of immigration laws. Michelle Malkin, author of *Invasion*, cites example after example of problems at the Immigration and Naturalization Service (INS).[55]

Foreign students getting visas to enter the U.S. constitute a major problem that is out of control. Malkin says that the bill establishing this new department doesn't do anything about it. There is also a problem with foreigners getting tourist visas to enter the U.S. and then overstaying their visas. The bill doesn't do anything about this problem either.

More than 115,000 people from Iraq and other Middle Eastern countries are here illegally. Some 6,000 Middle Eastern men who have defied deportation orders remain on the loose. Add these numbers to those who are here legally, but still intend harm to the United States, and you can begin to grasp the extent of the problem.

Consider the case of Hesham Mohamed Hedayet, who shot and killed people at the Los Angeles International Airport. He managed to stay in this country by obtaining a work permit after his wife won residency in a visa lottery program (given to 50,000 foreigners on a random basis).

---

[54] Lincoln Caplan, "Secret Affairs," *Legal Affairs*, Nov.-Dec. 2002, https://www.legalaffairs.org/issues/November-December-2002/affairs_novdec2002.msp

[55] Michelle Malkin, *Invasion: How America Still Welcomes Terrorists, Criminals, And Other Foreign Menaces To Our Shores* (Regnery, 2004).

Michelle Malkin broke the story about the Washington, D.C. area sniper suspect John Malvo. The INS had him in custody but released him. The U.S. State Department failed to obtain a warrant for the arrest of the other sniper suspect, John Muhammad after he was suspected of using a forged birth certificate to obtain a U.S. passport.

Congress needs to take another look at both the Patriot Act and the Homeland Security Act. In its rush to deal with the imminent terrorist threat, it has conferred broad powers to bureaucrats that should be refined and failed to address some crucial concerns in immigration that continue to threaten our safety. It is time for Congress to pass some common sense amendments to these two pieces of legislation.

History of Governmental Power

I think all of us would strongly support the President and Attorney General in their attempts to track down terrorists and bring them to justice. But some wonder if Congress has put too much power in the hands of the executive branch, power that could easily be abused by this administration or future administrations.

Let us consider our history. President John Adams used the Alien and Sedition Act to imprison his political enemies and curb newspaper editors critical of him. President Woodrow Wilson permitted his attorney general (Mitchell Palmer) to stop political dissent during the Palmer Raids. And President Franklin Delano Roosevelt interned thousands of Japanese-American citizens during World War II.

It is interesting that some of the greatest expansions of powers have come under Republican presidents. The first Republican president, Abraham Lincoln, suspended the writ of habeas corpus. (This is a judge's demand to bring a prisoner before him, with the intent to release people from unlawful detention.) This led to the imprisonment of physicians, lawyers, journalists, soldiers, farmers, and draft resisters. Sixteen members of the Maryland legislature were arrested in order to prevent them from voting for their state to secede from the Union. By the time the Civil War was over, 13,535 arrests had been made.

Although Democrats have often been credited with expanding the size and scope of the federal government, Republican administrations are actually the ones who have expanded various police powers. RICO and nearly all the seizure laws (where police can confiscate cars, boats, even homes without due process) were passed by Republican administrations.

Congress should revisit this important topic of anti-terrorism and modify some of the provisions of the Patriot Act. Some have suggested that Congress pass legislation that would sunset all aspects of the Patriot Act. The bill currently has sunset provisions that apply to selected portions of the legislation. But sunset provisions do not apply to the expanded powers given to the federal government that weakens the Fourth Amendment protections we are guaranteed under the Bill of Rights. The bill was touted as an emergency wartime measure, but some of the most dangerous aspects of the bill would continue on even after America wins the war on terrorism. It is time to revisit this bill and make some necessary changes.

Christian Perspective on Government and Privacy

Let's focus in on the matter of government and privacy. To begin with, Christians must acknowledge that Romans 13:1-7 teaches that civil government is divinely ordained by God. Government bears the sword, and that means it is responsible for protecting citizens from foreign invaders and from terrorists. So on the one hand, we should support efforts by our government to make our society safer.

On the other hand, we should also work to prevent unwarranted intrusions into our privacy and any violation of our constitutional liberties. In the past, drawing lines was easier because an unconstitutional search was conducted by a person who came to your door. Today we live in a cyber age where our privacy can be violated by a computer keystroke.

In the past, what used to be called public records weren't all that public. Now they are all too public. And what used to be considered private records are being made public at an alarming rate. What should we do?

First, live your life above reproach. Philippians 2:14-15 says "Do all things without grumbling or disputing, that you may prove yourselves to be blameless and innocent, children of God above reproach in the midst of a crooked and perverse generation, among whom you appear as lights in the world." 1 Timothy 3:2 says that an elder must be "above reproach" which is an attribute that should describe all of us. If you live a life of integrity, you don't have to be so concerned about what may be made public.

Second, get involved. When you feel your privacy has been violated or when you believe there has been an unwarranted governmental intrusion into your life, take the time to complain. Let the person, organization or governmental agency know your concerns.

Many people fail to apply the same rules of privacy and confidentiality on a computer that they do in real life. Your complaint might change a behavior and have a positive effect.

Third, call for your member of Congress to take another look at both the Patriot Act and the Homeland Security Act. In their rush to deal with the imminent terrorist threat, Congress may have expanded federal powers too much. Track congressional legislation and write letters. Citizens need to understand that many governmental policies pose a threat to our privacy. Bureaucrats and legislators are in the business of collecting information and will continue to do so unless we set appropriate limits.

Sadly, most Americans are unaware of the growing threats to their privacy posed by government and law enforcement. Eternal vigilance is the price of freedom. We need to strike a balance between fighting terrorism and protecting constitutional rights.

CHAPTER 6 Sins of Privacy

Privacy is a common word but often misunderstood because of its various meanings. We know when we feel that someone has violated our privacy, but we can't always give a definition to it, especially in this age in which new technology allows perpetrators to cross boundaries more easily than in the past.

David Holzman describes various ways we lose our privacy in his book, *Privacy Lost: How Technology is Endangering Your Privacy*.[56] He suggests that privacy violations can be viewed as seven sins ranging from intrusion to deception to profiling to identity theft. Let's look at each one of these sins against privacy he describes in his book.

1. <u>Sin of Intrusion</u> - The classical form of privacy abuse is intrusion. This "is the uninvited encroachment on a person's physical or virtual space." In previous ages, it took the form of voyeurism or peeping. Technology today allows for a much great intrusion into our lives and is often much more difficult to detect.

Radio Frequency Identification Devices (RFID) act like a wireless bar code and is being used more often in stores and other establishments (such as libraries) for inventory control. Geographic Positioning System (GPS) receivers are satellite locating devices that are found in cars, cell phones, and many other devices.

2. <u>Sin of Latency</u> - Most of the damage to your privacy comes from stored information. The harm is minimized if personal information is not retained. The sin of latency comes from the excessive hoarding of

---

[56] David Holzman, *Privacy Lost: How Technology is Endangering Your Privacy* (San Francisco: Josey-Bass, 2006).

information beyond an agreed-upon time. Most companies do not have a data aging policy.

It is understandable why companies and the government collect excessive information. First, they need to have enough information, so they know they have the right person. There are lots of John Smiths in a particular locality. They need to know you are the particular John Smith they want. In the past, a telephone number was sufficient identification. Now we have more than one phone and change numbers regularly. So our Social Security number and other identifiers are necessary.

A second reason for companies to collect information is so they can more effectively sell their products and services to you. They collect that information from the forms you fill out and even place cookies on your computer in order to catalog your visits to their Web site.

3. <u>Sin of Deception</u> - With so much electronic information available in databases, it is tempting for individuals, companies, and even bureaucrats to use personal information in a way that was not authorized by the person.

When a company or governmental agency asks for personal information, we should have the right to know three things: what they are going to do with it, how long they will keep it, and whether they will make it available to others. When we fill out a form for a credit card or enter into a contract for a car or house, we reveal lots of information. We may naively assume that they will be the only ones who will see that information. That is not so and a reason why we should be careful.

4. <u>Sin of Profiling</u> - Past behavior is not always a perfect predictor of future behavior, but it can be a surprisingly accurate one. That is where profiling comes in. Collecting information about what goods and services

someone purchases can enable companies to predict a consumer's future purchases.

Profiling is often used to predict more than that. David Holzman says that he worked with one credit card company that said: "it was able to pinpoint when its consumers were having life crises such a mid-life depression by psychographically analyzing their buying patterns."

Profiling is also used to fight terrorism, but have also caught innocent people in their profiling net. For some time my name was on a watchlist, and people like columnist Cal Thomas and Senator Ted Kennedy were on a no-fly list.

5. <u>Sin of Identity Theft</u> - Most of us know what identity theft is because it has happened to someone we know or else we have heard commercials about how to protect ourselves from identity theft. Although this crime did exist in the past, it has exploded on the scene now because of technology and the changing nature of transactions. Personal information is readily accessible on the Internet.

We may inadvertently give out that information. A phone call from someone pretending to be a bank executive can often elicit confidential information. "Phishing" is a mass e-mail with a message pretending to be a bank or brokerage. People who believe that it is genuine will enter information that the theft can use to drain their bank accounts.

6. <u>Sin of Outing</u> - Some privacy violations are deliberate and can take place when someone reveals information that another person would like to remain hidden. The term "outing" is usually used to describe a public revelation of a closet homosexual, but we can use the term to describe any information that is published about a person they do not want to be public.

Citizens, politicians, and even corporations have been the targets of Internet messages that have been used to damage their reputation. A number of court cases have attempted to force Web site managers to reveal the identities of those who are spreading false and libelous information.

Sometimes outing is a good thing. Think of all the potential pedophiles that have been caught because they thought they were chatting online with a potential underage victim. Sting operations by the police have successfully revealed the motives of some who intend to proposition their young victims.

7. <u>Sin of Lost Dignity</u> - This last concern is more difficult to quantify, but we all realize that when private information is made public, we can lose a part of our dignity. What if all of your medical records were made public? What if every essay you ever wrote in school was available online?

Even public figures (like politicians) believe they should have a zone of privacy. The Past and current presidents have refused to publish all of their medical records, school records, and other private information. While we may debate whether public figures should reveal all of this information, we would probably all agree that private citizens should not lose a zone of privacy in their lives.

SECTION 2 SOCIAL TRENDS

How is this rapidly changing world affecting me? What type of technological entertainment should I choose? How will this technology affect me personally and my relationship with God? How are these trends affecting my generation? Do these new technological trends help or harm my family?

CHAPTER 7 The Changing American Family

Are we headed toward a post-marital society where marriage is rare, and the traditional family is all but extinct? One would certainly think so by reading some of the stories that have appeared lately. A *New York Times* headline in 2003 warned of "marriage's stormy future" and documented the rise in the number of nontraditional unions as well as the rising percentage of people living alone.[57] A 2006 *New York Times* article documented the declining percentage of married couples as a proportion of American households and thus declared that married households are now a minority.[58] And a 2007 headline proclaimed that: "51% of women are now living without a spouse."[59]

Well, let us take a deep breath for a moment. To borrow a phrase from Mark Twain, rumors about the death of marriage and family are greatly exaggerated. But that doesn't mean that marriage as an institution is doing well and will continue to do well in the twenty-first century.

Let us first take on a few of these headlines pronouncing the end of marriage. The October 2006 *New York Times* headline concluded that: "To Be Married Means to Be Outnumbered." In other words, married households are now a minority in America and unmarried households are the majority. But the author

---

[57] Tamar Lewin, "Ideas & Trends: Untying the Knot: For Better or Worse: Marriage's Stormy Future," *New York Times*, 23 November 2003, 1.

[58] Sam Roberts, "It's Official: To be Married means to be Outnumbered," *New York Times*, 15 October 2006, 22.

[59] Sam Roberts, "51% of Women are now Living Without Spouse," *New York Times*, 16 January 2007, 1.

had to manipulate the numbers in order to come to that conclusion. This so-called "new majority" of unmarried households include many widows who were married. In addition, this claim only works if you count households and not individuals. For example, if you have two households—one with two married people and three children and another with a single widow living alone—they would be split between one married household and one unmarried household. However, one household has five people, and the other household has one person.

What about the January 2007 *New York Times* headline proclaiming that "51% of Women Are Now Living Without a Spouse"? Columnist and radio talk show host Michael Medved called this journalistic malpractice[60] and the ombudsman for the *New York Times* took his own paper to task for the article.[61] The most recent available figures showed that a clear majority (56%) of all women over the age of twenty are currently married.

So how did the author come to the opposite conclusion? It turns out that the author chose to count more than ten million girls between the ages of fifteen and nineteen as "women." So these so-called "women" are counted as women living without a spouse (never mind that they are really teenage girls living at home with their parents). This caused the ombudsman for the *New York Times* to ask this question in his op-ed: "Can a 15-year-old be a 'Woman Without a Spouse'?"[62]

---

[60] Michael Medved, "Journalistic Malpractice in 'Marriage is Dead' Report, 17 January 2007, www.townhall.com.

[61] Peter Smith, "New York Times Ombudsman Takes Place to Task for its Journalistic Midadventures on Marriage," 13 February 2007, www.LifeSiteNews.com.

[62] Byron Calame, "Can a 15-Year-Old Be a 'Woman Without a Spouse'?" New York Times, 11 February 2007.

It is also worth mentioning, that even with this statistical sleight of hand you still cannot get to the conclusion that a majority of women are living without a spouse. The article's author had to find a way to shave off an additional 2% of the married majority. He did this by including those women whose "husbands are working out of town, are in the military, or are institutionalized."[63]

Conflicting Attitudes about Marriage and Family

It is certainly premature to say that married couples are a minority and women living without a husband are a majority. But there has been a definite trend that we should not miss and will now address. The definition of marriage and the structure of family in the twenty-first century is very different from what existed in the recent past.

A few decades ago, marriages were the foundation of what many commentators referred to as "the traditional family." Now marriages and families are taking some very unfamiliar shapes and orientations due to different views of marriage and family.

Americans are not exactly sure what to think about these dramatic changes in marriage and family. On the one hand, they believe that marriage and family are very important.

A *Better Homes and Garden* survey found that their readers rated their relationship to their spouse as the single most important factor in their personal happiness.[64] And a MassMutual study on family values (taken many years ago) reported that eight out of ten Americans

---

[63] Roberts, "51% of Women are now Living Without Spouse."
[64] *What's Happening to American Families*, October 1988. 22.

reported that their families were the greatest source of pleasure in their lives, more than friends, religion, recreation, or work.[65]

On the other hand, Americans are much less sanguine about other people's marriages and families. I call this the "Lake Wobegon effect" where "all the women are strong, all the men are good-looking, and all the children are about average." In other words, *their* marriage and family are fine, but the rest of the marriages and families are *not*. While the MassMutual Family Values Study found that a majority (81%) pointed to their family as the greatest source of pleasure, it also found that a majority (56%) rated the family in the U.S. "only fair" or "poor." And almost six in ten expected it to get *worse* in the next ten years. The survey concluded that: "Americans seem to see the family in decline everywhere but in their own home."[66]

Similar results can be found in many other nationwide polls. A Gallup poll found that Americans believe the family is worse off today than it was ten years ago. And they believed it would be worse off in the future as well.[67] Americans also demonstrated their ambivalence toward marriage and family not only in their attitudes but their actions. One trend watcher predicted more than a decade ago in an article in *American Demographics* that marriage would become in the 1990s and the twenty-first century "an optional lifestyle."[68]

---

[65] *MassMutual American Values Study*, July 1989.

[66] Ibid., 29-30.

[67] "The 21st Century Family," *Newsweek Special Edition*, Winter/Spring 1990, 18.

[68] Martha Farnsworth Riche, "The Postmarital Society," *American Demographics*, November 1988, 23.

Changing Trends in Marriage

While it may be too early to put the institution of marriage on the endangered species list, there is good reason to believe that changing attitudes and actions have significantly transformed marriage in the twenty-first century. The current generations are marrying later, marrying less, and divorcing more than previous generations.

A major transition in attitudes toward marriage began with the baby boom generation. From 1946 to 1964, over seventy-six million babies were born. By the 1960s the leading edge of the baby boom generation was coming of age and entering into the years when previous generations would begin to marry. But baby boomers (as well as later generations) did not marry as early as previous generations. Instead, they postponed marriage until they established their careers. From the 1960s to the end of the twenty-first century, the median age of first marriage increased by nearly four years for men and four years for women.

Some of those who postponed marriage ended up postponing marriage indefinitely. An increasing proportion of the population adopted this "marriage is optional" perspective and never married. They may have had a number of live-in relationships, but they never joined the ranks of those who married. For them, singleness was not a transition but a lifestyle.

Over the last few decades, the U.S. Census Bureau has documented the increasing percentage of people who fit into the category of "adults living alone." These are often lumped into a larger category of "non-family households." Within this larger category are singles that are living alone as well as a growing number of unmarried, cohabiting couples who are "living together." The U.S. Census Bureau estimated that in 2000 there were nearly ten million Americans living with an unmarried opposite-sex partner and another 1.2 million Americans living with a same-sex partner.

These numbers are unprecedented. It is estimated that during most of the 1960s and 1970s, only about a half a million Americans were living together. And by 1980, that number was just 1.5 million.[69] Now that number is more than twelve million.

Cohabiting couples are also changing the nature of marriage. Researchers estimate that half of Americans will cohabit at one time or another prior to marriage.[70] And this arrangement often includes children. The traditional stereotype of two young, childless people living together is not completely accurate; currently, some 40% of cohabiting relationships involve children.[71]

Couples often use cohabitation to delay or forego marriage. But not only are they postponing future marriage, but they are also increasing their chance of marriage failure. Sociologists David Popenoe and Barbara Dafoe Whitehead, in their study for the National Marriage Project, wrote: "Cohabitation is replacing marriage as the first living together experience for young men and women." They conclude that those who live together before they get married are putting their future marriage in danger.[72]

---

[69] U. S. Bureau of the Census, *Current Population Reports*, Series P20-537; America's Families and Living Arrangements: March 2000 and earlier reports.

[70] Larry L. Bumpass, James A. Sweet, and Andrew Cherlin, "The Role of Cohabitation in the Declining Rates of Marriage," *Journal of Marriage and Family* 53 (1991), 914.

[71] Ibid., 926.

[72] David Popenoe and Barbara Dafoe Whitehead, "Should We Live Together? What Young Adults Need to Know about Cohabitation before Marriage," *The National Marriage Project*, the Next Generation Series, Rutgers, the State University of New Jersey, January 1999.

Finally, we should note the impact of cohabitation on divorce. When the divorce rate began to level off and even slightly decline in the 1980s, those concerned about the state of marriage in America began to cheer. But soon the cheers turned to groans when it became obvious that the leveling of the divorce rate was due primarily to an increase in cohabitation. Essentially the divorce rate was down because the marriage rate was down. Couples who break up before they marry don't show up as divorce statistics.

Many marriages today are less permanent than in previous decades. There have always been divorces in this country, but what used to be rare has now become routine. Changing attitudes toward marriage and divorce in this country are reflected in the changing divorce rate.

A graph of the divorce rate shows two significant trends. One is a sharp increase in divorces in the late 1960s that continued through the 1970s. The second is a leveling and even a slight decline in the 1980s. Both are related to the attitudes of the baby boom generation toward marriage and divorce.

The increasing divorce rate in the 1970s was due to both attitude and opportunity. Baby boomers did not stay married as long as their parents due to their different attitudes towards marriage and especially their attitude toward commitment in marriage. It is clear from the social research that the increase in the divorce rate in the 1970s did not come from empty nesters (e.g., builders) finally filing for divorce after sending their children into the world. Instead, it came from young couples (e.g., baby boomers) divorcing even before they had children.[73]

---

[73] Landon Jones, *Great Expectations: America and the Baby Boom Generation* (New York: Ballantine, 1980), 215.

The opportunity for divorce was also significant. When increasing numbers of couples began seeking a divorce, state legislatures responded by passing no-fault divorce laws. Essentially a married person could get a divorce for any reason or no reason at all.

Economic opportunity was also a significant factor in divorce. During this same period, women enjoyed greater economic opportunities in the job market. Women with paychecks are less likely to stay in a marriage that was not fulfilling to them and has less incentive to stay in a marriage. Sociologist David Popenoe surveying a number of studies on divorce concluded that "nearly all have reached the same general conclusion. It has typically been found that the probability of divorce goes up the higher the wife's income and the closer that income is to her husband's."[74]

The second part of a graph on divorce shows a leveling and even a slight decline. The divorce rate peaked in 1981 and has been in decline ever since. The reasons are twofold. Initially, the decline had to do with the aging of the baby boom generation who were entering into those years that have traditionally had lower rates of divorce. But long term the reason is due to what we have already discussed in terms of the impact of cohabitation on divorce. Fewer couples are untying the knot because *fewer couples are tying the knot*.

Changing Trends in Family

We have already mentioned that starting with the baby boom generation and continuing on with subsequent generations, couples postponed marriage. But not only did these generations postpone marriage, but they also postponed procreation. Unlike the generations

---

[74] David Popenoe, *Disturbing the Nest: Family Change and Decline in Modern Societies* (New York: de Gruyter, 1988), 223.

that preceded them (e.g., the builder generation born before the end of World War II), these subsequent generations waited longer to have children and also had few children. Lifestyle choice was certainly one factor. Another important factor was cost. The estimated cost of raising a child during this period of time rose to over six figures. Parents of a baby born in 1979 could expect to pay $66,000 to rear a child to eighteen. For a baby born in 1988, parents could expect to pay $150,000, and that did not include additional costs of piano lessons, summer camp, or a college education.[75] Now the estimated cost is nearly $250,000.[76]

When these generations did have children, often the family structure was very different than in previous generations. Consider the impact of divorce. Children in homes where a divorce has occurred are cut off from one of the parents, and they suffer emotionally, educationally, and economically.

Judith Wallerstein in her research discovered long-term psychological devastation to the children.[77] For example, three out of five children felt rejected by at least one parent. And five years after their parents' divorce, more than one-third of the children were doing markedly worse than they had been before the divorce. Essentially she found that these emotional tremors register on the psychological Richter scale many years after the divorce.

The middle class in this country has been rocked by the one-two punch of divorce and illegitimacy, creating

---

[75] Karen Peters, "$150,000 to Raise a Kid," *USA Today*, 17 January 1990, 1A.

[76] Lam Thuy Vo, "How Much Does it Cost to Raise a Child?, *Wall Street Journal*, 22 June 2016.

[77] Judith Wallerstein and Sandra Blakeslee, *Second Chances: Men, Women and Children A Decade after Divorce* (New York: Ticknor and Fields, 1989).

what has been called the "feminization of poverty." U.S. Census Bureau statistics show that single moms are five times more likely to be poor than are their married sisters.[78]

An increasing percentage of women give birth to children out of wedlock. This increase is due in large part to changing attitudes toward marriage and family. In a society that is already changing traditional patterns (by postponing marriage, divorcing more frequently, etc.), it is not surprising that many women are avoiding marriage altogether. Essentially, the current generation disconnects having children and getting married. In their minds, they separate parenthood from marriage, thus creating an enormous increase in the number of single-parent homes.

Greater social acceptance of out-of-wedlock births, divorce, and single parenting tends to reinforce the trends and suggests that these percentages will increase in the future. Young adults who contemplate marriage may be less inclined to do so because they were raised in a home where divorce occurred. A young woman raised by a single mom may be less inclined to marry when they are older, convinced that they can raise a child without the help of a husband. Better employment options for young women even encourage them to "go it alone."

These changes in attitudes and changes in the structure of marriage and family have created a very different family in the twenty-first century. One writer imagined the confusion that children would feel in this futuristic scenario:

> On a spring afternoon, half a century from today, the Joneses are gathered to sing "Happy Birthday" to Junior. There's Dad and his third

---

[78] Bureau of the Census, *Statistical Abstract of the United States*, 1992 (Washington, DC: U.S. Government Printing Office, 1993), Table 719.

wife, Mom and her second husband, Junior's two half brothers from his father's first marriage, his six stepsisters from his mother's spouse's previous unions, 100-year-old Great Grandpa, all eight of Junior's current "grandparents," assorted aunts, uncles-in-law and step cousins. While one robot scoops up the gift wrappings and another blows out the candles, Junior makes a wish . . . that he didn't have so many relatives.[79]

---

[79] "When the Family Will Have a New Definition," *What the Next 50 Years Will Bring*, a special edition of *U.S. News and World Report*, 9 May 1983, A3.

CHAPTER 8 Exponential Times

You may have seen the YouTube video asking, "Did you know"? Sometimes it has the title "We are living in exponential times." I want to look at some of the trends that illustrate the fact that we live in exponential times. While I will use the video as a starting point, I will also be citing other authors and commentators as well.

The video begins by talking about population. How often we forget that there are countries like China and India that have a billion people. For example, the video says that if you are one in a million in China, there are thirteen hundred other people just like you. That is because there are over a billion people in China.

The video also points out that twenty-five percent of India's population with the highest IQs is actually greater than the total population of America. Put another way, India has more honors kids than America has kids.

This reminds me of a statement in *The World Is Flat* by Thomas Friedman. He says that when he was growing up his parents would tell him "Finish your dinner. People in China and India are starving." Today he tells his daughters, "Girls, finish your homework—people in China and India are starving for your jobs."[80]

Consider the population explosion. There were one billion people in 1800. We did not reach two billion until 1930. The planet had three billion people in 1960 and four billion in 1975. We reached five billion people in 1987 and six billion people in 1999. It is estimated that the planet will hold seven billion people in 2012.

Of course, life expectancy has been going up, and this is changing the demographic of various countries.

---

[80] Thomas Friedman, *The World is Flat: A Brief History of the Twenty-First Century* (New York: Farrar, Straus and Giroux, 2005), 237.

Many more people are living to age 100 and beyond. For example, there were only two hundred centenarians in France in 1950. The number is projected to reach a hundred fifty thousand by the year 2050. That is a seven-hundred-fifty-fold increase in one hundred years.[81]

Alternatively, consider the United States population increase in this demographic group. In 1990, there were approximately, thirty thousand centenarians. Some believe that estimate may be a bit too high, but it provides an approximate baseline. The U.S. Census Bureau estimates there will be two hundred sixty-five thousand centenarians by 2050.[82]

One last trend is that world population growth is slowing down as populations are aging. Demographers tell us that we need 2.1 children per woman to replace a population. Back in the 1950s, the average number of babies per woman of childbearing age was 5.0 but has been dropping ever since. It will most likely reach 2.3 in 2025.[83]

In the developing world, fertility is already moderately low at 2.58 children per woman and is expected to decline further to 1.92 children per woman by mid-century.[84] While only three countries were below the population replacement level of 2.1 babies in 1955, there will be one hundred and two such countries by 2025.[85]

---

[81] "50 Facts: Global health situation and trends," World Health Organization, 1998.

[82] "Centenarians in the United States," U.S. Census Bureau, 1999.

[83] "50 Facts: Global health situation and trends."

[84] "World population to increase by 2.6 billion over next 45 years," World Population Prospects, 24 February 2005.

[85] "50 Facts: Global health situation and trends."

Exponential Growth

What is the impact of exponential growth on society? Richard Swenson argues in his book *Margin* that this has created unprecedented problems for us:

> One major reason our problems today are unprecedented is because the mathematics are different. Many of the linear lines that in the past described our lives well have now disappeared. Replacing them are lines that slope upward exponentially.[86]

Exponential growth is very different from arithmetic growth. We live our lives in a linear way. We live day-to-day, week-to-week, month-to-month. But the changes taking place around us are increasing not in a linear way but in an exponential way.

Exponential growth is not something that we would consider intuitive. Scott Armstrong demonstrated that when he asked a graduate class of business students the following question. If you folded a piece of paper in half forty times, how thick would it be? Most of the students guessed it would be less than a foot. A few guessed it would be greater than a foot but less than a mile. Two students guessed it would be great than a mile but less than two thousand miles. The correct answer is that the paper would be thick enough to reach from here to the moon.[87]

This is the challenge of living in exponential times. If the graph is linear, we have a fairly good grasp of what that will mean for us in the future. When the graph

---

[86] Richard Swenson, *Margin: How to Create the Emotional, Physical, Financial, and Time Reserves You Need* (Colorado Springs: NavPress, 1992), 44.

[87] Scott Armstrong, *Long-Range Forecasting: From Crystal Ball to Computer* (NY: Wiley, 1985), 102.

curves upward exponentially, we have a difficult time comprehending its impact.

But will the graph continue to trend upward? It will until it reaches some limit.

Eventually, there is an upper limit to most of the trends we are seeing. Objective things (people, government buildings, and organizations) have limits. Subjective things (relationships, creativity, and spirituality) also have limits.

At this point, the curve changes from a J-curve to an S-curve. The exponential slope begins to flatten and reach a new equilibrium. Eventually, there is a turning point at which the upward curve no longer grows exponentially. Finally, the curve levels as growth and limits reach an equilibrium.

One of the challenges of living in exponential times is that the various trends are at different points on the curve. The amount of new information seems to be exploding exponentially and looks like a J-curve. The number of e-mails you receive might not be growing exponentially like it did a few years ago but may still be increasing. Population in many developing countries has been leveling off (and often decreasing), and so the graph looks more like the S-curve. All of these trends are at different parts of the curve and are happening simultaneously. Thus, it is often difficult for us to comprehend what this means to us personally.

Futurists who are trying to understand what will happen in the future are faced with an even more daunting task. If they look at each trend in isolation, they can begin to get an idea of what might happen. But as soon as someone tries to integrate all of these trends into a comprehensive whole, the future becomes blurred.

Trying to integrate all the various trends (many growing exponentially) creates a challenge for anyone trying to accurately predict the future. We might know the individual trends, but trying to integrate hundreds of trends into a comprehensive picture is difficult, if not impossible.

Warnings About Exponential Growth

In the past, a number of authors have warned about the dangers of exponential growth. And because their predictions did not come to pass, the concept of exponentiality and its impact have faded from current discussion.

In the early nineteenth century, Thomas Malthus wrote his famous *Essay on the Principle of Population* in which he argued that population growth would outstrip food production. He reasoned that population would grow exponentially while food production would merely grow arithmetically. Thus, he predicted a future crisis due to this exponential growth.

In 1968, Stanford biologist Paul Ehrlich published his controversial best-seller, *The Population Bomb*. He also noted that population was growing exponentially and made numerous predictions about catastrophes that would befall the human race in the 1970s and 1980s.

Dennis Meadows and others with a group known as The Club of Rome published their report in the book *The Limits to Growth*. The authors used a computer simulation to consider the interaction of five variables (world population, industrialization, pollution, food production and resource depletion). By changing the various assumptions about population and resources, they predicted various dire scenarios for the future.

Of course, these doomsday predictions never came to pass. Therefore, it was inevitable that discussion and warning about exponential growth were no longer published on the front pages of newspapers and newsmagazines.

Another reason we have ignored the potential impact of exponential growth is due to the remarkable technological achievements of the twentieth century. Automobile manufacturers have been able to significantly increase gas mileage in cars. Petroleum engineers have been able to find more effective and efficient ways to pull oil from the ground. Farmers and scientists have essentially tripled global food production since World War II, thereby outpacing even population growth.

Nevertheless, there are indeed limits to growth. If we understand what those limits are and work within them, then the future will be bright. If we ignore them, the human race could be in for some rough times. Harvard biologist E.O. Wilson expressed this dichotomy when he asked, "Are we racing to the brink of an abyss, or are we just gathering speed for a takeoff to a wonderful future? The crystal ball is clouded; the human condition baffles all the more because it is both unprecedented and bizarre, almost beyond understanding."[88]

Columnist Tom Harper is more pessimistic: "Currently we are behaving like insane passengers on a jet plane who are busy taking all the rivets and bolts out of the craft as it flies along."[89]

Whatever our future, it is certain that is will be more complex than ever before. And it will be a world in which information has exploded exponentially.

---

[88] E.O Wilson, "Is Humanity Suicidal?" *The New York Times Magazine*, 30 May 1993, 27.

[89] Tom Harper, quoted by William Goetz, *Apocalypse Next: The End of Civilization as We Know It?* (Camp Hill, PA: Horizon Books, 1996), 15.

Information Explosion

One aspect of exponential times is the information explosion. The YouTube video by the same title reminds us that information is exploding exponentially. For example, it points out that there are thirty-one billion searches on Google every month. The best estimate is now there are about thirty-six billion searches on Google each month. In 2006, it was 2.7 billion. That's a thirteen-fold increase in just three years.

In order to keep up with this information explosion, engineers have been working at a breakneck pace to increase the efficiency and capacity of computers and other devices that process and store information. Every year, fifty quadrillion transistors are produced. That is more than six million for every human on the planet.[90]

Look at the exponential growth of Internet devices. In 1984, there were a thousand. By 1992, there were one million. By 2008, there were one billion and the number is about to exceed two billion. Some experts believe that there will be fifteen billion Intelligent Connected Devices by the year 2015.[91]

The YouTube video estimates that a week's worth of *The New York Times* contains more information than a person was likely to come across in a lifetime in the eighteenth century. This figure is more difficult to quantify even though it, or variations of it, is cited all the time.

In fact, this may be our biggest challenge in the twenty-first century. There is so much information that most of us are having a difficult time trying to make sense

---

[90] George Gilder, "Happy Birthday Wired: It's Been a Weird Five Years," *Wired*, January 1998, 40.

[91] "15 Billion Connected Devices – Powered by the Embedded Internet," Small Forms Factors Blog, 28 April 2009.

of all the data. Facts, figures, and statistics are coming at us at an accelerating rate. That is why we need to evaluate everything we see, read, and hear from a Christian worldview in order to make sense of the world around us.

One last point is that most of this information is still in the English language. The YouTube video says that there are about 540,000 words in the English language. And this is five times as many words as in the time of Shakespeare.

It turns out that these estimates may be a bit off. Part of the problem is deciding what constitutes a word. After all, we have so many derivatives of a word and we have many words that have multiple meanings. Do you count the word or the various meanings of a word?

Let us start with the English vocabulary at the time of Shakespeare. We know how many words he used. If you count all the words in his plays and sonnets, there are 884,647 of them. The estimate for the number of different words he used varies from eighteen to twenty-five thousand. I might also mention that it appears that Shakespeare coined or invented about fifteen hundred new words. Even so, it seems like the estimate that there were a hundred thousand English words in Shakespeare's time might be too high.

Do we have over five hundred thousand words in the English language today? Again, it depends on how you count words. The largest English dictionary has about four hundred thousand entries. A more realistic number is around two hundred thousand. The latest edition of the *Oxford English Dictionary* contains entries for 171,476 words in current use and 47,156 obsolete words.

Nevertheless, English has become the language of choice for the world. Approximately three hundred seventy-five million people speak English as their first language. Another seven hundred million speak English as a foreign language. English is also the language most often studied as a foreign language in the European Union. English is more widely spoken and written than any other language.

English is the medium for eighty percent of information stored in the world's computers. English is the most common language used in the sciences as well as on the Internet. Not only have the number of English words expanded since Shakespeare's time, but its influence has also expanded as well.

Exponential Times and a Biblical Worldview

The Bible tells us that we are to understand the times in which we are living. First Chronicles 12:32 says that the sons of Issachar were "men who understood the times, with knowledge of what Israel should do." Likewise, we need to understand our times with knowledge of what we as Christians should do.

We have also been looking to the future by trying to plot trends from today into tomorrow. The Bible also tells us that we should plan for the future. Isaiah 32:8 says that "the noble man devises noble plans, and by noble plans, he stands." Proverbs 16:9 says "the mind of man plans his way, but the Lord directs his steps." So we should not only plan for the future but commit those plans to the Lord and be sensitive to His leading in our lives.

When you live in a world that is increasing exponentially, you have to be ready for change. In fact, it is probably true that most of us now expect change rather than stability in our world. Not so long ago, there were those telling us that change would shock our senses and disorient us.

As commentator Mark Steyn points out, we developed a whole intellectual class of worriers. He says:

> The Western world has delivered more wealth and more comfort to more of its citizens than any other civilization in history, and in return we've developed a great cult of worrying. You know the classics of the genre: In 1968, in his bestselling book *The Population Bomb*, the eminent scientist Paul Ehrlich declared: "In the 1970s the world will undergo famines—hundreds of millions of people are going to starve to death." In 1972, in their landmark study *The Limits to Growth*, the Club of Rome announced that the world would run out of gold by 1981, of mercury by 1985, tin by 1987, zinc by 1990, petroleum by 1992, and copper, lead and gas by 1993.[92]

Obviously none of that happened. But we shouldn't dismiss the potential impact of exponential growth, but learn to be more careful in our predictions.

I believe one of the greatest challenges for Christians will come from the information explosion. Not only are we inundated with facts, figures, and statistics, but we must also confront various philosophies, worldviews, and religions. It is absolutely essential that Christian develop discernment. We must work to evaluate everything we see, read, and hear from a Christian worldview.

---

[92] Mark Steyn, "It's the Demography Stupid," *Wall Street Journal*, 4 January 2006.

CHAPTER 9 Baby Boomerangs

In the last few years, newspapers and newsmagazines have been full of stories about baby boomers and baby busters returning to church. Is there a spiritual revival taking place? What caused the exodus and what is bringing about the return? These are just a few questions we will address.[93]

When the baby boomers began returning to church, they were dubbed "baby boomerangs." A similar phenomenon has now been observed for the baby boomers. Most of them grew up in religious households. In fact, about 96 percent had some religious instruction in their early years. But many jettisoned their religious beliefs when they became adults because spirituality seemed irrelevant in the secular, pluralistic culture of modern life. Now, like boomerangs return to the point of their departure, many baby boomers are returning to church.

At least two processes were responsible for their exodus from organized religion. The process of secularization in modern society removed religious ideas and institutions from the dominant place they had in previous generations. Religious ideas were less meaningful, and religious institutions were more marginal in their influence on the baby boom generation. To their parents' dismay, most boomers dropped out of traditional religion for at least two years during their adolescence and adulthood.

The process of pluralization in their world rapidly multiplied the number of worldviews, faiths, and ideologies. This increase in choice led naturally to a decrease in commitment and continuity. Many boomers

---

[93] Most of the material in this chapter is taken from my book *Signs of Warning, Signs of Hope* (Moody, 1994).

and busters during their adolescence and early adulthood went through what might be best called serial-conversions. Spiritually hungry for meaning, they dined heartily at America's cafeteria for alternative religions: est, gestalt, meditation, scientology, bioenergetics, and the New Age. Others sought spiritual peace through 12-step programs for alcoholics, workaholics, even chocoholics. This have-it-your-way, salad-bar spirituality has been high on choices and options but low on spiritual commitment.

One author wrote, "Although there are those who try to follow the demanding precepts of traditional religion, most baby boomers find refreshment in a vague religiosity which does not interfere in any way with how they live."[94]

As this generation passes through midlife, it will inevitably look to the future more with anxiety than anticipation. Boomers and busters are asking, Who will care for me? Will I be able to provide for my family and me?

And these questions are also mingled with questions of identity. Who am I? Where am I going? Is this all there is to life? These questions have an underlying spiritual dimension and are not easily answered in a secular world nor in a mystical world filled with bland spirituality.

Certainly, this generation has sought answers in self-help programs and community activities, but something more than social changes and technology is necessary. As one commentator said, "There is a feeling of being lost and looking for something greater. People know that technology has not worked for them. It hasn't done anything for their souls."

---

[94] George Sim Johnston, "Break Glass in Case of Emergency," *Beyond the Boom: New Voices on American Life, Culture, and Politics*, ed. Terry Teachout (New York: Poseidon, 1990), 55.

This is, in part, why many baby boomers and baby busters have begun to return to church. But is this a true spiritual revival? Furthermore, what about the large segment of this generation that is still outside the church and seemingly uninterested in coming back? What could the church do to reach out to those boomers who are still outside the church?

Seekers of Experiences

As in other endeavors, baby boomers and baby busters have been seekers: seekers of pleasure, seekers of experience, seekers of freedom, seekers of wealth, and yes, seekers of spirituality. But unlike their parents, boomers' search for spirituality took them down unpredictable paths. This generation has been eclectic in its religious experiences where brand loyalty is unheard of and the customer is king. While some have stayed true to the "faith of their fathers," most mix traditional religion with New Age mysticism and modern self-help psychologies in a flexible and syncretistic manner.

Boomers and busters can be divided into three religious subcultures: loyalists, returnees, and dropouts. Loyalists tend to be social conservatives. They had better relations with their parents and tended to grow up in stricter homes. Loyalists never really identified with the counterculture and never left their church or synagogue.

At the other extreme are the dropouts. They had less confidence in the country when growing up and had more conflicts with parents. Traditional religion was, to them, out of touch with modern life. They have never come back to church and pursue spirituality (if at all) in a personal and individual way.

Between the loyalists and the dropouts are the returnees. They were and are middle-of-the-road types who were less alienated than the dropouts but more disaffected than the loyalists. They left church or synagogue and have returned but often with some ambivalence.

Each religious subculture manifests differences in spiritual styles and commitment but all are affected to some degree by their experiences in the counterculture. Though their views are different from one another, collectively the three boomer subcultures are very different from their parents. For example, few in the returnees subculture actually consider themselves religious and do not hold to traditional views of God even though they may actually attend religious services on a regular basis. Returnees are much less likely to engage in traditional religious activities (daily prayers, saying grace at meals, reading the Bible). Almost one-fourth of returnees and nearly one-fifth of loyalists say they believe in reincarnation.

In short, boomers and busters are very different from their parents in terms of spiritual commitment and biblical understanding. And churches and Christian organizations that reach out to this generation must be aware of these differences if they are to be effective.

Boomers, Busters, and Their Children

Those boomers and busters who have returned to church—the so-called "baby boomerangs"—have returned for one of two major reasons: children or spiritual restlessness. Boomers concerned about the moral and spiritual upbringing of their children have made the spiritual pilgrimage back to their religious roots. Members of this generation may say they do not believe in absolute values, but frequently their relativistic worldview collapses when they have children. They don't want their kids growing up without any moral direction. Church suddenly becomes a much more important place. Gallup surveys, for example, show that nearly nine in ten Americans say they want religious training for their kids, even though fewer than seven in ten with children (ages 4-18) say they are currently providing such training.

The boomerang phenomenon is not peculiar to baby boomers and baby busters. Church historians have found a predictable pattern of church attendance that has affected numerous generations. Typically after high school, young adults drop out of church and often don't drop back into church until they have children. In that regard, boomers are no different than generations that preceded them.

Unlike previous generations, boomers and busters prolonged the cycle by postponing marriage and children. Getting married later and having children later essentially extended their absence from church. And this extended absence allowed many of them to get more set in their ways. A generation used to free weekends and sleeping in on Sunday is less like to make church attendance a priority.

Kids begin to rearrange those priorities. Statistically, it has been shown that the presence of children in a family makes a significant difference in the likelihood of church attendance. One survey found that married baby boomers are nearly three times more likely to return to church if they have children. Children do indeed seem to be leading their parents back to church.

Another reason for boomers and busters returning to church is spiritual restlessness. Sixteen hundred years ago, St. Augustine acknowledged, "We were made for thee, O God, and our hearts are restless until they find rest in thee." Social commentators have generally underestimated the impact of this generation's restless desire for meaning and significance. Ken Woodward, religion editor for *Newsweek* magazine, believes "That search for meaning is a powerful motivation to return to the pews. In the throes of a midlife re-evaluation, Ecclesiastes–'A time for everything under heaven'–is suddenly relevant."[95] George Gallup has found that two-thirds of those who dropped out of a traditional church (left for two years or more) returned because they "felt an inner need" to go back and rediscover their religious faith.

For these and other less significant reasons, baby boomers and baby busters are returning to church though not in the numbers sometimes reported in the media. All of this attention to returning boomers fails to take into account that more than forty percent of baby boomers have not returned to church. And while many are celebrating those coming in the front door, they shouldn't overlook the stream of boomers leaving the church out the back door. They are bored, disillusioned, or restless and need to be reached more effectively if the church is to make a difference in the 21st Century.

Skeptical of Society

Although much has been made of the baby boomerang phenomenon, many more are skeptical of church as well as other institutions such as government, military, and schools. While they are consistent with previous generations in their boomerang cycle, "statistics on church attendance, when viewed up close, reveal dramatic and distinctive patterns along generational lines." The data show:

- Throughout their lives, Americans born during the Depression have been more faithful than later generations in their church/synagogue attendance.

---

[95] Ken Woodward, "A Time to Seek," *Newsweek*, 17 Dec. 1990. 51.

- "War babies" [born 1939-45] dropped out of church as they entered their twenties during the turbulent sixties, and stayed away. The twin disillusionments stemming from Vietnam and Watergate made them more suspicious of institutions—the church included. Only recently, as they approach and pass midlife, are they trickling back to church.

- "Baby boomers" [born 1946-64] also dropped out of the church in their twenties, but now, in their thirties and early forties, they are returning to the ranks of the faithful. The real boom in church attendance is coming from this generation.[96]

Nevertheless, boomers and busters have been returning to church in increasing numbers.

Will this revitalized interest in religion make a difference in society? This is a question many social commentators are considering. "Will the churches and synagogues provide the kind of training necessary to keep the faith vital—or will the churches merely mirror the culture?" asks sociologist Os Guinness. "The natural tendency of the baby boomers is to be laissez faire socially. Will their return to faith make any decisive difference in their personal and social ethics, or will their religious commitment be [simply] a variant of their social philosophy?"[97]

Traditionally boomers and busters have been samplers with little brand loyalty. They don't feel bound to the denomination of their youth and search for experiences (both spiritual and otherwise) that meet their needs. It is not uncommon for families to attend different

---

[96] Wesley Pippert, "A Generation Warms to Religion," *Christianity Today*, 6 October 1989, p. 22.
[97] Ibid.

churches each week (or on the same day) to meet their perceived spiritual needs. They aren't bashful about attending a particular church to take advantage of a special seminar or program and then picking up and moving to another church when those programs seem inviting.

Many boomers and busters may be interested in spiritual issues but see no need to attend church. George Gallup refers to this characteristic in his book *The Unchurched in America–Faith Without Fellowship*. Such religious individualism stems both from American individualism that has been a part of this country for centuries and this generation's desire for flexibility and individuality. The have-it-your-way attitude in every area of a boomer's life has given rise to this religious individualism.

Boomers and busters approach religion and spirituality differently than previous generations. They embrace a faith that is low on commitment and high on choice. As one commentator noted, "They are comfortable with a vague, elastic faith that expands to fill the world after a pleasant Christmas service and contracts to nothing when confronted with difficulties." No wonder many boomers are starting to embrace religious beliefs that previous generations would never have considered.

Spiritual Hunger

Spiritually hungry boomers looking for nourishment for their souls have already tried a variety of selections from America's spiritual cafeteria. They will probably continue to do so. Lonely, isolated in boxes in the suburbs, often hundreds of miles from their families, boomers are facing significant psychological issues in the midst of busy lives that sap their emotional and spiritual resources. Beneath this isolation and turmoil is a restless desire for spirituality.

Some will try to meet these needs by dabbling in the New Age Movement. And if the churches do not meet their real and perceived needs, this trickle may turn into a torrent. The New Age Movement is attractive to the spiritually naive and institutionally cynical. If the church fails, then the New Age will thrive.

This may be the greatest challenge for the Christian church. Can church leaders woo them back to the flock? Can the church challenge boomers to a greater level of religious commitment in their lives? Can the church provide the religious training necessary to keep their faith vital? These are important questions.

Churches need to challenge them to deeper faith and greater religious commitment, but surveys and statistics show that churches themselves may be suffering from the same maladies as baby boomers. Church members like to believe that they are more spiritually committed and live lives different from the unchurched. The data show otherwise.

Approximately 40 percent of America attends church or other religious services on a fairly regular basis. But George Gallup has found that fewer than 10 percent of Americans are deeply committed Christians. Those who are committed "are a breed apart. They are more tolerant of people of diverse backgrounds. They are more involved in charitable activities. They are more involved in practical Christianity. They are absolutely committed to prayer."[98]

Numerous surveys show that most Americans who profess Christianity don't know the basic teachings of the

---

[98] "Fewer Than 10% of Americans Are Deeply Committed Christians," *National and International Religious Report*, 20 May 1991.

faith. Such shallow spirituality makes them more susceptible to the latest fad, trend, or religious cult. Gallup notes that not being grounded in the faith means they "are open for anything that comes along." For example, studies show that New Age beliefs "are just as strong among traditionally religious people as among those who are not traditionally religious."[99]

Lack of commitment to a faith position and to a lifestyle based on biblical principles also extends to church attendance and instruction. Eight in ten Americans believe they can arrive at their own religious views without the help of the church.

Commitment to biblical instruction is not high either. George Gallup says that Americans are trying to do the impossible by "being Christians without the Bible." He goes on to say that, "We revere the Bible, but we don't read it."[100] Pastors and pollsters alike have been astounded by the level of biblical illiteracy in this nation.

Churches that reach out to baby boomers and baby busters will have to shore up their own spiritual commitment as they challenge this generation to a higher level of commitment and discipleship. If they are successful, then their congregations will grow. If they aren't then this generation will go elsewhere to satisfy its spiritual hunger.

---

[99] Ibid.

[100] "Gallup Tells Editors: Americans Revere the Bible, Don't Read It," *World*, 19 May 1990.

CHAPTER 10 Midlife Transition

Each year more millions of Americans turn 40. Now there is nothing magical about turning 40 per se, but turning 40 does signal the beginning of a time of introspection and re-evaluation that generally occurs during the 40-something years.

Millions of people will encounter a mid-life transition in the 1990s. Why does this occur? How does it affect people? And how can Christians marshall the emotional and spiritual resources to deal with these changes? These are just a few of the questions we will address and attempt to answer.

The leading edge of the baby boom was the first group to hit this time of transition. Born in the late '40s and early '50s, they lived in new houses, built on new streets, in new neighborhoods, in the new American communities known as the suburbs.

When they headed off to school, they sat in new desks and were taught about Dick and Jane by teachers fresh out of college. They grew up with television and lived in a world brimming with promise. In the '60s they graduated from high school and enrolled in college in record numbers. Then they landed jobs at good salaries in a still-expanding economy and bought homes before housing prices and interest rates went through the roof.

Unlike the boomers and busters born after them, the leading edge boomers achieved, in large part, the American dream. They weren't smarter or more talented. Their success was due simply to being born earlier. But even though they have achieved a degree of financial success, many are beginning to encounter a crisis of purpose. They are like the cartoon that appeared in *The New Yorker*. The husband turns to his wife over the breakfast table and says, "The egg timer is pinging. The toaster is popping. The coffee pot is perking. Is this it, Alice? Is this the great American dream?"[101]

Millions will no doubt repeat these questions in the next few decades. Is this it? Is this the great American dream? Add to these questions others like: Where is my life going? Is this all I am ever going to achieve?

In some ways, these are strange questions coming from people who enjoy the fruits of the American economy. They have achieved a measure of success and yet they are asking questions that signal a coming crisis of purpose.

The Age 40 Transition

As each generation enters mid-life, it begins to reevaluate its values. Often they reject the values of their parents. They have also changed the structure of their families in ways that are unimaginable to previous generations. But they must now shoulder adult responsibilities and assume positions of leadership (if they aren't already in them). Put another way: the baby boom stands at a point of transition. This is not the first time this generation has collectively faced a point of transition. When the leading-edge boomers began turning 30, they hit what psychologist Daniel Levinson calls the "Age 30 Transition."[102] The struggle of leaving childhood and entering the adult years was worked out in a period of stagnant wages and appreciating house prices. Ultimately the collective angst of the boom generation turned Gail Sheehy's book *Passages: Predictable Crises of Adult Life*

---

[101] Cartoon reprinted in article by Daniel B. Moskowitz, "The Trappings of Success—Or Just a Trap?" *Business Week*, 6 February 1989.

[102] Daniel J. Levinson, et. al., *The Seasons of a Man's Life* (New York: Knopf, 1978).

into a runaway bestseller.[103] Among other things, the book assured people in midlife that they were not alone in their confrontation with a major life stage.

The leading edge of this generation is now in the midst of a more significant transition: the mid-life transition. Turning 40 is no more a predictor of change than turning 30 was. But somewhere in that time period, mid-life re-evaluation begins. It is a stage in which men and women begin to evaluate and question their priorities and deal with their dreams and aspirations.

While this transition is both somber and serious, some have attempted to inject some levity into the discussion. Lawyer Ron Katz found the YUPPIE designation an inaccurate description of his friends' lifestyle. So he coined, somewhat facetiously, yet another acronym to describe boomers at this stage. No longer rolling stones, but not yet the grateful dead, they're MOSS—middle-age, overstressed, semi-affluent suburbanites.

According to Katz, MOSS (or MOSSY, if you prefer the adjective) is what YUPPIES have become in the 1990s. As Katz says, a MOSS is "41 years old; more overstressed than overworked; affluent but doesn't feel that way." A MOSS also is beginning to understand why the world hasn't changed more over the past 25 years; [and] hopes that the world changes somewhat less over the next 30 years.

And while some social commentators want to discount the existence of a mid-life crisis, psychologists, and sociologists assure us that something is indeed taking place. It is not merely media hype or self-fulfilling prophecy. During the years of mid-life, a substantial re-evaluation is taking place.

---

[103] Gail Sheehy, *Passages: Predictable Crises of Adult Life* (New York: Bantam, 1974).

In actuality, the transition to mid-life is gradual. There are no major landmarks or signposts that signal our entry into this new and uncharted domain. Perhaps that is why there are so many jokes about turning 40 even though nothing of any significance actually happens on one's 40th birthday. Turning 40 provides a visible demarcation of a gradual process.

The Seasons of a Man's Life

In the preface of his book *The Seasons of a Man's Life*, Daniel Levinson says, "Adults hope that life begins at 40–but the great anxiety is that it ends there."[104] Fearing this may be true, many begin to become "frantic at forty-something." They are making a transition from the years of their youth to a time of adulthood without any hope or optimism.

In his book, Daniel Levinson describes a number of developmental stages in adult life. He delineates an early adult era from the mid-20s to the late 30s. He also discusses a middle adult era from the mid-40s to the early 60s. What is in-between is what he calls the years of mid-life transition. He sees these years as a bridge between young adulthood and senior membership in one's occupational world.

The psychological study done by Levinson focused on men between the ages of 35 and 45. He found that about 80 percent of those studied went through a time of personal crisis and re-evaluation during this mid-life transition. Levinson argued that the 20 percent that did not encounter a struggle were in a state of denial and would go through this transition later. This raises the first of two assumptions in these studies.

---

[104] Levinson, *The Seasons of a Man's Life*, ix.

While the stages and themes documented by these studies are descriptive, they are by no means normative. As a Christian, I reject a deterministic model that predicts everyone will go through a certain stage. While writing an earlier book on the subject of death and dying, I found that not all people go through the same psychological stages of grief. Christians, for example, who have come to terms with their own mortality and the mortality of their loved ones can face death and agree with the apostle Paul that it is better "to be absent from the body and present with the Lord" (1 Cor. 5:3). Likewise, people who have come to grips with their place in the world may not face a wrenching mid-life crisis.

A second assumption has to do with the subjects of these studies. The major studies of adult development (including Levinson's study) used male subjects born before the 1930 depression. Comparable studies for women were not done, and studies of baby boomers have not been done.

The men in the study have at least three things in common. They grew up in stable families; they had realistic goals for their lives; and they became adults in an expanding economy. Few experienced divorces in their families. Most had simple goals like "being able to provide for their families" and "being a good father." They also built their careers in a flourishing economic climate.

These assumptions are not true for the baby boom generation. They grew up in less-stable families and now are raising families in a world where divorce is very common. Baby boomers have much greater expectations and thus have personal goals that are much more difficult to fulfill. And baby boomers reached adulthood when the economy was shrinking.

Such differences make it difficult to apply these studies directly to the boom generation. While some investigators argue that talk about a true mid-life "crisis" is overblown, most believe the current generation will be even more susceptible to a crisis than the previous one.

New Roles

In his research, Levinson discovered a number of themes that surface during the time of mid-life transition. The first is that mid-life transition involves adapting to new roles and responsibilities. By the time you are in your 30s, you are expected to think and behave like a parent. You can postpone this for a while, and the boom generation has been fairly successful at postponing adulthood by extending the period simply called "youth."

Boomers extended adolescence into their 20s and even into their 30s. Now they are facing different and more demanding sets of roles and expectations. They are taking senior positions in their jobs and must provide care for both their children and their aging parents.

A man in his 40s is usually regarded by people in their 20s as a full generation removed. He is seen more as a parent than as a brother. In the minds of those who are younger, he is "Dad" rather than "buddy." This message comes first as a surprise and then as an irritation to a man in mid-life.[105]

Another way to look at this transition is to use the definitions of generations used by Spanish philosopher Jos Ortega y Gasset. He identifies five generations: childhood, youth, initiation, dominance, and old age.

The Initiation generation includes the time of mid-life transition and leads to what he calls the Dominant Generation, where individuals are expected to assume the mantle of leadership, authority, and responsibility.

---

[105] Ibid., 28.

According to Ortega y Gasset, the Initiation and Dominant generations are the two most crucial ones. The relations between them and the successful passing of authority from one to another affect the fate of society. During the 1990s and the early part of the 21st century, this transition from the older generation to the younger generation will be taking place.

Mortality

The second stage of mid-life transition involves dealing with our own mortality. In mid-life we become increasingly aware of death. Living in a death-denying culture shields us from a sense of our own mortality. And being young further heightens our sense of indestructibility. Teenagers and young adults tend to think of themselves as "bullet-proof" and destined for immortality. But by the age of 40, we have seen many people not much older than ourselves succumb to cancer and heart attacks. Many of us have seen death in our own families. The death of a parent is a clear signal that we are now on our own. It also reminds us how short life really is.

People going through this transition not only face a crisis of mortality; they face a crisis of growing old. People in midlife enter what I call the "Ache Age." Vigorous exercise is followed by hurting muscles that seem to stay sore longer. Cuts and bruises that used to heal almost overnight take much longer to heal. Such physiological reminders also focus our attention on our own mortality.

Dr. Elisabeth Kubler-Ross has identified five different stages of grief. Although these describe the psychological stages of a patient who is dying, they correlate remarkably well with the feelings people go through in mid-life. Whether it is the death of an individual or the death of their dreams, the emotional feelings are often the same.

Culminating Events

A mid-life transition surfaces from a culminating event. This event serves as a marker for a conclusion of young adulthood. It may be a very obvious one like a promotion or being fired from a job. But it also might be something that no one would be able to identify, not even our spouses. It is a milestone that helps us see that one of our life's dreams is not going to be realized, and it provides an estimate for future success or fulfillment.

In *The Seasons of a Man's Life*, Daniel Levinson argues that the dreams we have are so compelling that nothing short of total success will satisfy. In other words, there is no such thing as modest success. Frequently, the culminating event is seen as evidence of flawed success and often as a total failure.

To those on the outside looking in, a man may seem like he has reached the pinnacle of success. But they can't see into his irrational mind affected by sin. He may have dreams that are hopelessly unrealistic, especially in youth.

It may be that a man is the president of a very successful company but nevertheless feels like a failure because his dream was to be President of the United States. A man who is very athletic and runs marathons feels unfulfilled because his dream was to play in the NBA. A woman who is one of the top salespeople in the company may feel inadequate because she wanted a family and cannot have kids.

Intense Introspection

Fourth, mid-life transition involves intense introspection. A consistent pattern of adult life is an early struggle in adulthood to achieve a measure of success followed by a mid-life appraisal of one's values and philosophy of life. A man around 40 begins to reassess the meaning of life and begins reconsidering the fate of his youthful dreams. He is asking major questions like: Is this all I am going to do the rest of my life? Is this all I am going to achieve?

Many people find that what they thought was going to make them happy isn't making them happy. They enjoyed law school and the first few years of law. But the thought of practicing law for the rest of their life is not very fulfilling. They enjoyed the first few years selling life insurance, but the thought of selling insurance for another 30 years sounds more like torture than a career.

This is a time when an individual shines a light on his or her accomplishments and sets an agenda for the second half of life. There may or may not be major mid-course corrections depending on the evaluation.

Leaving a Legacy

Finally, a mid-life transition involves leaving a legacy. As we come to grips with our own mortality, we inevitably desire immortality, which is "one of the strongest and least malleable of human motives." Leaving a legacy means finding a form of immortality by leaving something behind. One is reminded of Woody Allen's quip that he didn't want to be immortal by leaving something behind; he wanted to be immortal by not dying. But since that is not possible, then an individual seeks to leave a legacy, and that quest usually forms the core of the second half of a person's life.

Successful resolution of mid-life comes from determining what legacy–possessions, memories, ministry–we will leave behind. The legacy may encompass family, work, or all of society. It may involve contributions as a parent, spouse, leader, or mentor. These elements of the legacy define the path we will take in the second half of our lives.

Application

These then are the basic themes of the mid-life transition. For the Christian, there are two points of application. First is a personal application. If you are going through mid-life, recognize that you are going to be in a daily battle over three issues.

First, you will have a daily battle with your thoughts. We need to "take every thought captive to the obedience of Christ" (2 Corinthians 10:5). We will also have a daily battle with temptation. A key verse to memorize is 1 Corinthians 10:13. And finally, we will have a daily battle with sin and must confess our sins (1 John 1:8-9).

The second point of application is to our personal ministry. If we are attentive to this mid-life transition, we will be able to minister to millions of people who will go through this struggle. The 1990s might be the greatest time for harvest in this generation. Until now, most baby boomers have had few struggles. As they confront mid-life, many will be asking important questions that can lead to evangelistic opportunities.

Here are two ways you can help. First, a knowledge of the transition can ease the struggle. Daniel Levinson says knowing the transition is coming is an important antidote to its effects. So a knowledge of this transition can help you reach out.

Second, a knowledge of the Bible can help you to minister. A generation that has been impervious to the gospel may be more willing to listen as it asks the fundamental questions of life. If we reach out in love with a biblical message, we can make a difference.

CHAPTER 11 Time and Busyness

It has, perhaps, always been true that "time is money." But for the current generation, this maxim has a new twist. In the frenetic 21st century, time has become even scarcer than money and therefore more valuable. As with any commodity, the law of supply and demand determines value. In the last few decades, free time has grown scarce and hence has become a valuable possession.

We now live in the decade of the time famine. Leisure time, once plentiful and elastic, is now scarce and elusive. People seeking the good life are finding it increasingly difficult to enjoy it, even if they can afford it. What money was in the past, time has become today.

According to one survey, the amount of leisure time enjoyed by the average American has shrunk 37 percent since 1973. A major reason is an expanding workweek. Over this same period, the average workweek (including commuting) has increased from fewer than 41 hours to nearly 47 hours. And in many professions, such as medicine, law, and accounting, an 80-hour week is not uncommon. The survey, therefore, concludes that "time may have become the most precious commodity in the land."[106]

The Technology of Time

Our current time crunch has caught most people off-guard. Optimistic futurists in the 1950s and 60s, with visions of utopia dancing in their heads, predicted Americans would enjoy ample hours of leisure by the turn of the century. Computers, satellites, and robotics

---

[106] Nancy Gibbs, "How America Has Run Out of Time," Time, 24 April 1989, 58.

would remove the menial aspects of labor and deliver abundant opportunities for rest and recreation.

The optimists were partly right: computers crunch data at unimaginable speeds, orbiting satellites cover the globe with a dizzying array of messages, and robots zap together everything from cars to computer chips at speeds far exceeding their human counterparts. Yet these and other technological feats have not freed Americans from their labors. Most people are busier than ever.

It wasn't supposed to be this way. Testimony before a Senate subcommittee in 1967 predicted that "by 1985, people could be working just 22 hours a week or 27 weeks a year or could retire at 38."[107] The major challenge facing people in the 1990s should have been what to do with all the leisure time provided by our technological wizardry.

Instead, technology has been more of an enemy than an ally. "Technology is increasing the heartbeat," says Manhattan architect James Trunzo, who designs automated environments. "We are inundated with information. The mind can't handle it all. The pace is so fast now, I sometimes feel like a gunfighter dodging bullets."[108]

Actually, the problem isn't so much technology as it is the heightened expectations engendered by it. The increased speed and efficiency of appliances, computers, and other machines have enabled us to accomplish much more than was possible in previous decades. But this efficiency has also fostered a desire to take on additional responsibilities and thereby squeeze even more activities into already crammed calendars.

---

[107] Laurence Shames, *The Hunger for More* (New York: Time Books, 1989), 35.
[108] Quoted in Ibid.

As the pace of our lives has increased, over-commitment and busyness have been elevated to socially desirable standards. Being busy is chic and trendy. Pity the poor person who has an organized life and a livable schedule. Everyone, it seems, is running out of time.

Time-Controlling Devices

It is little wonder that most of the products now being developed are not so much time-savers as they are time-controllers. Most of the appliances developed in the 1950s–vacuum cleaners, dishwashers, mixers–were designed to save time and remove drudgery from housework. By comparison, most of the products developed in the last few decades–answering machines, voicemail, automatic tellers–were time- controllers. These devices do not save much time, but they do allow harried consumers to use their time more effectively.

Technological efficiency has also increased competition. Labor- saving devices that are supposed to make life easier frequently force people to work harder. Baby boomers who are intensely competing with one another for jobs and prestigious promotions avidly employ the latest equipment to give them an edge. Faxes, LANs, car phones, and laptop computers are viewed as necessities if one is to remain competitive.

But technology isn't enough. So most professionals, especially those in service industries such as law, accounting, and advertising, work long hours in an effort to meet their clients' seemingly endless needs and demands. Other baby boomers feel trapped in the same rat race because economic pressures make it nearly impossible to support a family on one income.

The work ethic seems out of control. In the frenetic dash for success or just plain survival, leisure time becomes a scarce commodity. "My wife and I were sitting on the beach in Anguilla on one of our rare vacations," recalls architect James Trunzo, "and even there my staff was able to reach me. There are times when our lives are clearly leading us."

No Time to Talk

Everywhere, it seems, people are over-scheduled and over-committed. Workers are weary. Parents are preoccupied. And children and family relationships are often neglected.

A survey by Cynthia Langham at the University of Detroit found that parents and children spend only 14.5 minutes per day talking to each other.[109] That is less time than a football quarter and certainly much less time than most people spend commuting to work.

She says that many people are shocked to hear the 14.5-minutes statistic. But once they take a stopwatch to their conversations, they realize she is right.

But that 14.5 minute statistic is misleading since most of that time is squandered on chitchat like "What's for supper?" and "Have you finished your homework?" Truly meaningful communication between parent and child, unfortunately, occupies only about two minutes each day. Langham concludes, "Nothing indicates that parent-child communications are improving. If things are changing, it's for the worse."

She points to two major reasons for this communication breakdown. First is a change in the workforce. A few decades ago, the dinner table was a forum for family business and communication. But now, when dinner time rolls around, Dad is still at work, Mom is headed for a business meeting, and sister has to eat and

---

[109] Quoted in Leslie Barker, "We Never Seem to Talk Any More," *Dallas Morning News*, 25 September 1989, C-1.

run to make it to her part-time job. Even when everyone is home, there are constant interruptions to meaningful communication.

The second reason for poor parent-child communication is the greatest interruption of all: television. Urie Bronfenbrenner of Cornell has reported a forty-year decline in the amount of time children spend with their parents, and much of the recent loss is due to television. TV sabotages much of the already-limited time families spend together. Meals are frequently eaten in front of the "electronic fireplace." After dinner, talk-starved families gather to watch congenial television families with good communication skills.

While some television shows deal with issues families might discuss (drugs, pregnancy, honesty), few families take advantage of these opportunities to talk about the dilemmas portrayed on the programs and provide moral instruction.

The greeting card business has developed a whole new product line for busy parents and children. More and more children are finding cards in their backpacks or under their pillows that proclaim, "Have a good day at school," or lament, "I wish I were there to tuck you in."

The effect of time pressures on the family has been devastating. Yale psychology professor Edward Ziglar somberly warns that: "as a society, we're at the breaking point as far as family is concerned."

Homemaking and child-rearing are full-time activities. When both husband and wife work, maintaining a home and raising a family becomes difficult. In the increasing numbers of single-parent households, the task becomes next to impossible.

Someone has to drive car pools, make lunches, do laundry, cope with sick kids and broken appliances, and pay the bills. In progressive homes, household tasks are shared as the traditional husband/wife division of labor breaks down. In others, super-Mom is expected to step into the gap and perform flawlessly.

Inevitably, children are forced to grow up quickly and take on responsibilities they should never have to shoulder. Some children are effectively abandoned–if not physically, at least emotionally- -and must grow up on their own. Others are latchkey kids who are forced to mature emotionally beyond their years. These demands take their toll and create what sociologist David Elkin has called the "hurried child" syndrome.[110]

Time, or rather our lack of it, is severely hurting families. Nurturing suffers when families do not have time to communicate, and parents do not have time to instruct their children. In the end, the lack of time takes its toll on the stability of our families.

Never Enough Time

One survey done by *Family Circle* documented the loss of time in families, especially for working mothers. The article, entitled "Never Enough Time?" began: "Remember 'quality time'? In the 1980's that was what you sandwiched in for the children between the office and the housework. We all learned how valuable time was in the school of hard knocks. Life was what happened while we were busy making other plans, to paraphrase ex-Beatle John Lennon." That was then.[111]

A resounding 71 percent of those surveyed said their lives had gotten busier in the previous year. Nearly a third attributed this increase in busyness to expanding

---

[110] David Elkin, *The Hurried Child* (Reading, MA: Addison-Wesley, 1981).

[111] Stephanie Abarbanel and Karen Peterson, "Never Enough Time? You Can Beat the Clock," *Family Circle*, 14 March 1989, 115.

workloads at the office, the demands of a new job, or the pressures of starting a business or returning to work. Not only were the women working longer hours, but many were also working on weekends, and nearly a third often took work home.[112]

Dual-income couples reported major difficulties finding time for each other. Negotiating schedules and calendar juggling were daily activities. Three out of four women in the survey reported that finding enough time to be alone with their husbands was "often" or "sometimes" a major stress in their relationships.[113] When asked, "In a time crunch, who gets put on the back burner?" half said friends, then husbands, and then other family members.

Those hit hardest by time pressures were single parents. One single mother with two teenagers in Illinois wrote: "I am responsible for a house and yard, work 40 hours a week, take college classes, run a local support group for divorced and widowed women and am involved with a retreat group through church. I have time because I *make* time."[114]

Often the first thing women will let slide is housekeeping. A full 82 percent said they had changed their standards of cleaning and organizing a house. When asked why 49 percent said other things are more important, 42 percent said they were more relaxed about letting chores wait, 35 percent said they had one or more young children, and 23 percent said they had taken a paying job.

The time pressure on women and families is significant. The time crunch is squeezing out meaningful communication and important time to think and reflect.

---

[112] Ibid.
[113] Ibid., 116.
[114] Ibid., 119.

The additional time will not come without changes in our lifestyles.

Redeeming the Time

Time, or the lack of it, will continue to dominate our thinking through the 1990s. All of us are in the midst of a time crunch–the solution is to recognize our priorities and apply them rigorously to our lives.

First, we must establish biblical priorities in our lives. Often our busyness is merely a symptom of a deeper problem, such as materialism. In Luke 12, Jesus illustrated this danger with the parable of the rich fool. He says, "The land of a certain rich man was very productive. And he began reasoning to himself, saying, `What shall I do, since I have no place to store my crops?' And he said, `This is what I will do: I will tear down my barns and build larger ones, and there I will store all my grain and my goods. And I will say to my soul, "Soul, you have many goods, laid up for many years to come; take your ease, eat, drink and be merry."' But God said to him, `You fool! This very night your soul is required of you; and now who will own what you have prepared?'"

There are a number of applications we can derive from this passage. First, we should make sure that we are not so involved in the affairs of the world that we neglect the affairs of the spirit. To turn the familiar adage around, we can be so earthly-minded we are no heavenly good.

Second, we should ask ourselves if we are tearing down productive resources for a more luxurious lifestyle. If a three-bedroom house is sufficient, are we selling it merely to move up to a four- bedroom house? If the car we are currently driving is fine, are we nevertheless eager to trade it in on a newer or more expensive model?

Often our indulgences constrain our time and financial resources.

This observation leads to our second biblical principle: fight materialism in our lives. Proverbs 28:20 says "He who makes haste to be rich will not go unpunished." Materialism brings with it a haste to get rich. Materialistic people are not patient people. They want what they want, when they want it, and they want it now.

Often our lack of time is tied to our haste to get rich, to feed our greed. We need to ask ourselves the fundamental question, How much do we really need? If we fight materialism in our lives and cut back on the lavishness of our lifestyle, we might be surprised how much time we will free up.

A third biblical principle is to redeem the time. Ephesians 5:15-16 says "Therefore be careful how you walk, not as unwise men, but as wise, making the most of your time, because the days are evil." Colossians 4:5 says, "Conduct yourselves with wisdom toward outsiders, redeeming the time."

Unlike many of the other resources God has given us, time is not renewable. We may lose money, but we can always earn more. We may lose our possessions, but we can always acquire new ones. But time is a non-renewable commodity. If we squander our time, it is lost forever.

All of us, but especially Christians, must carefully manage the time that God has given us. It is a valuable resource, and we can either spend it on ourselves or redeem it as a spiritual investment. We can spend it only once, and how we spend it can have eternal consequences. Let us not waste the resources God has given us. Instead, let us redeem the time and use it for God's glory.

CHAPTER 12 Loneliness

The postwar generations are headed for a crisis of loneliness. The reasons are simple: demographics and social isolation. More of them are living alone than in previous generations, and those living with another person will still feel the nagging pangs of loneliness.[115]

In previous centuries where extended families dominated the social landscape, a sizeable proportion of adults living alone was unthinkable. And even in this century, adults living alone have usually been found near the beginning (singles) and end (widows) of adult life. But these periods of living alone are now longer due to lifestyle choices on the front end and advances in modern medicine on the back end.

People are postponing marriage and thus extending the number of years of being single. Moreover, their parents are (and presumably they will be) living longer, thereby increasing the number of years one adult will be living alone. Yet the increase in the number of adults living alone originates from more than just changes at the beginning and end of adult life. Increasing numbers are living most of their adult lives alone.

In the 1950s, about one in every ten households had only one person in them. These were primarily widows. But today, due to the three D's of social statistics (death, divorce, and deferred marriage), about one in every four households is a single person household. And if current trends continue, sociologists predict that ratio will increase to one in every three households by the twenty-first century.

---

[115] A more extensive discussion of loneliness can be found in my book, *Signs of Warning, Signs of Hope* (Chicago: Moody, 1994).

In the past, gender differences have been significant in determining the number of adults living alone. For example, young single households are more likely to be men, since women marry younger. On the other hand, old single households are more likely to be women, because women live longer than men. While these trends still hold true, the gender distinctions are blurring as boomers of both sexes reject the traditional attitudes towards marriage. Compared with their parents, boomers are marrying less, marrying later, and staying married for shorter periods of time.

Marriage Patterns

The most marriageable generation in history did not make the trip to the altar in the same percentage as their parents. In 1946, the parents of the baby boom set an all-time record of 2,291,000 marriages. This record was not broken during the late 1960s and early 1970s when millions of boomers entered the marriage-prone years. Finally, in 1979, the record that had lasted 33 years was finally broken when the children of the baby boom made 2,317,000 marriages.

Instead of marrying, many boomers chose merely to "live together." When this generation entered the traditional years of marriageability, the number of unmarried couples living together in the United States doubled in just ten years to well over a million. The sharpest change was among cohabiting couples under 25, who increased ninefold after 1970. Demographers estimate that there have been as many as one-and-a-half to two million cohabiting couples in the U.S. Yet even high figures underestimate the lifestyle changes of boomers. These figures merely represent the number of couples living together at any one time. Cohabitation is a fluid state, so the total number living together or living alone is in the millions.

Not only is this generation marrying less; they are also marrying later. Until the baby boom generation arrived on the scene, the median age of marriage remained stable. But since the mid-fifties, the median age of first marriage has been edging up. Now both "men and women are marrying a full eighteen months later than their counterparts a generation earlier."

Another reason for a crisis in loneliness is marital stability. Not only is this generation marrying less and marrying later; they also stay married less than their parents. The baby boom generation has the highest divorce rate of any generation in history. But this is only part of the statistical picture. Not only do they divorce more often; they divorce earlier. When the divorce rate shot up in the sixties and seventies, the increase did not come from empty nesters finally filing for divorce after sending their children into the world. Instead, it came from young couples divorcing before they even had children. Demographer Tobert Michael of Stanford calculated that while men and women in their twenties comprised only about 20 percent of the population, they contributed 60 percent of the growth in the divorce rate in the sixties and early seventies.[116]

The crisis of loneliness will affect more than just the increasing number of people living alone. While the increase in adults living alone is staggering and unprecedented, these numbers are fractional compared with the number in relationships that leave them feeling very much alone.

Commitment is a foreign concept to most of the million-plus cohabiting couples. These fluid and highly mobile situations form more often out of convenience and demonstrate little of the commitment necessary to make a relationship work. These relationships are

---

[116] Landon Jones, *Great Expectations: America and the Baby Boom Generation* (New York: Ballantine, 1980), 215.

transitory and form and dissolve with alarming frequency. Anyone looking for intimacy and commitment will not find them in these relationships.

Commitment is also a problem in marriages. Spawned in the streams of sexual freedom and multiple lifestyle options, boomers may be less committed to making a marriage work than previous generations. Marriages, which are supposed to be the source of stability and intimacy, often produce uncertainty and isolation.

Living-Together Loneliness

Psychologist and best-selling author Dan Kiley has coined the term "living-together loneliness," or LTL, to describe this phenomenon. He has estimated that 10 to 20 million people (primarily women) suffer from "living together loneliness."[117]

LTL is an affliction of the individual, not the relationship, though that may be troubled too. Instead, Dan Kiley believes LTL has more to do with two issues: the changing roles of men and women and the crisis of expectations. In the last few decades, especially following the rise of the modern feminist movement, expectations that men have of women and that women have of men have been significantly altered. When these expectations do not match reality, disappointment (and eventually loneliness) sets in. Dan Kiley first noted this phenomenon among his female patients in 1970. He began to realize that loneliness comes in two varieties. The first is the loneliness felt by single, shy people who have no friends. The second is more elusive because it involves the person in a relationship who nevertheless feels isolated and very much alone.

---

[117] Dan Kiley, *Living Together, Feeling Alone: Healing Your Hidden Loneliness* (New York: Prentice-Hall, 1989).

According to Kiley, "There is nothing in any diagnostic or statistical manual about this. I found out about it by listening to people."[118] He has discovered that some men have similar feelings, but most tend to be women. The typical LTL sufferer is a woman between the ages of 33 and 46, married and living a comfortable life. She may have children. She blames her husband or live-in partner for her loneliness. Often he's critical, demanding, uncommunicative. The typical LTL woman realizes she is becoming obsessed with her bitterness and is often in counseling for depression or anxiety. She is frequently isolated and feels some estrangement from other people, even close friends. Sometimes she will have a fantasy about her partner dying, believing that her loneliness will end if that man is out of her life.

To determine if a woman is a victim of LTL, Kiley employs a variation of an "uncoupled loneliness" scale devised by researchers at the University of California at Los Angeles. For example, an LTL woman would agree with the following propositions: (1) I can't turn to him when I feel bad, (2) I feel left out of his life, (3) I feel isolated from him, even when he's in the same room, (4) I am unhappy being shut off from him, (5) No one really knows me well.

Kiley also documents five identifiable stages of LTL which are likely to affect baby boom women. A typical LTL woman who marries at about age 22 will feel bewildered until she is 28. At that point, isolation sets in. At 34, she begins to feel agitated. This turns to depression between the ages of 43 and 50. After that, a woman faces absolute exhaustion.

---

[118] Dixie Reed, "Alone Together, " *Dallas Times Herald*, 20 Nov. 1989, B-1,3.

Women may soon find that loneliness has become a part of their lives whether they are living alone or "in a relationship," because loneliness is more a state of mind than it is a social situation. People who find themselves trapped in a relationship may be more lonely than a person living alone. The fundamental issue is whether they reach out and develop strong relationship bonds.

Male Loneliness

In recent years, social psychologists have expressed concern about the friendless male. Many studies have concluded that women have better relational skills which help them to be more successful at making and keeping friends. Women, for example, are more likely than men to express their emotions and display empathy and compassion in response to the emotions of others. Men, on the other hand, are frequently more isolated and competitive and therefore have fewer (if any) close friends.

Men, in fact, may not even be conscious of their loneliness and isolation. In his book *The Hazards of Being Male: The Myth of Masculine Privilege*, Herb Goldberg asked adult men if they had any close friends. Most of them seemed surprised by the question and usually responded, "No, why? Should I?"[119]

David Smith lists in his book *Men Without Friends* the following six characteristics of men which prove to be barriers to friendship.[120] First, men show an aversion to showing emotions. Expressing feelings is generally taboo for males. At a young age, boys receive the cultural message that they are to be strong and stoic.

---

[119] Herb Goldberg, *The Hazards of Being Male: The Myth of Masculine Privilege* (New York: New American Library, 1976).

[120] David W. Smith, *Men Without Friends* (Nashville: Thomas Nelson, 1990), 24-30.

As men, they shun emotions. Such an aversion makes deep relationships difficult, thus men find it difficult to make and keep friendships.

Second, men seemingly have an inherent inability to fellowship. In fact, men find it hard to accept the fact that they need fellowship. If someone suggests lunch, it is often followed by the response, "Sure, what's up?" Men may get together for business, sports, or recreation (hunting and fishing), but they rarely do so just to enjoy each other's company. Centering a meeting around an activity is not bad, it is just that the conversation often never moves beyond work or sports to deeper levels.

Third, men have inadequate role models. The macho male image prevents strong friendships since a mask of aggressiveness and strength keeps men from knowing themselves and others. A fourth barrier is male competition. Men are inordinately competitive. Men feel they must excel in what they do. Yet this competitive spirit is frequently a barrier to friendship.

Fifth is an inability to ask for help. Men rarely ask for help because they perceive it as a sign of weakness. Others simply don't want to burden their family or colleagues with their problems. In the end, male attempts at self-sufficiency rob them of fulfilling relationships.

A final barrier is incorrect priorities. Men often have a distorted order of priorities in which physical things are more important than relationships. Success and status is determined by material wealth rather than by the number of close friends.

Men tend to limit their friendships and thus their own identity. H. Norman Wright warns:

> The more a man centers his identity in just one phase of his life—such as vocation, family, or career—the more vulnerable he is to threats against his identity and the more prone he is to experience a personal crisis. A

man who has limited sources of identity is potentially the most fragile. Men need to broaden their basis for identity. They need to see themselves in several roles rather than just a teacher, just a salesman, just a handsome, strong male, just a husband.

Crowded Loneliness

Loneliness, it turns out, is not just a problem of the individual. Loneliness is endemic to our modern, urban society. In rural communities, although the farm houses are far apart, community is usually very strong. Yet in our urban and suburban communities today, people are physically very close to each other but emotionally very distant from each other. Close proximity does not translate into a close community.

Dr. Roberta Hestenes at Eastern College has referred to this as "crowded loneliness." She says:

> Today we are seeing the breakdown of natural "community" network groups in neighborhoods like relatives, PTA, etc. At the same time, we have relationships with so many people. Twenty percent of the American population moves each year. If they think they are moving, they won't put down roots. People don't know how to reach out and touch people. This combination produces crowded loneliness.[121]

Another reason for social isolation is the American desire for privacy. Though many boomers desire community and long for a greater intimacy with other members of their generation, they will choose privacy even if it means a nagging loneliness. Ralph Keyes, in his

---

[121] Quoted in Dennis Rainey, Lonely Husbands, Lonely Wives (Dallas: Word, 1989), 11-12

book *We the Lonely People*, says that above all else Americans value mobility, privacy, and convenience.[122] These three values make developing a sense of community almost impossible. In his book *A Nation of Strangers*, Vance Packard argued that the mobility of American society contributed to social isolation and loneliness. He described five forms of uprooting that were creating greater distances between people.[123]

First is the uprooting of people who move again and again. An old Carole King song asked the question, "Doesn't anybody stay in one place any more?" At the time when Packard wrote the book, he estimated that the average American would move about 14 times in his lifetime. By contrast, he estimated that the average Japanese would move five times.

The second is the uprooting that occurs when communities undergo an upheaval. The accelerated population growth during the baby boom along with urban renewal and flight to the suburbs have been disruptive to previously stable communities.

Third, there is the uprooting from housing changes within communities. The proliferation of multiple-dwelling units in urban areas crowd people together who frequently live side by side in anonymity.

The fourth is the increasing isolation due to work schedules. When continuous-operation plants and offices dominate an area's economy, neighbors remain strangers.

And fifth, there is the accelerating fragmentation of the family. The steady rise in the number of broken families and the segmentation of the older population from the younger heightens social isolation. In a very real

---

[122] Ralph Keyes, *We the Lonely People*, quoted in Smith, *Men Without Friends*, 169.

[123] Vance Packard, *A Nation of Strangers* (New York: David McKay, 1972), 2-5.

sense, a crisis in relationships precipitates a crisis in loneliness.

Taken together, these various aspects of loneliness paint a chilling picture of the 1990s. But they also present a strategic opportunity for the church. Loneliness will be on the increase in this decade, and Christians have an opportunity to minister to people cut off from normal, healthy relationships.

The local church should provide opportunities for outreach and fellowship in their communities. Individual Christians must reach out to lonely people and become their friends. And ultimately we must help a lost, lonely world realize that their best friend of all is Jesus Christ.

CHAPTER 13 The Millennial Generation

The Millennial generation is a group of young people whose birth years range from 1980 to 2000. This generation is actually just slightly larger than the Baby Boom generation (born from 1946 to 1964). Nearly 78 million Millennials were born between 1980 and 2000.

Millennials are already having an impact on business, the workplace, churches, and other organizations. They certainly are having an impact on politics. The 18- to 29-year-old Millennials voted for Barack Obama in 2008 by a significant margin. Because of their impact in business, politics, and the church, they are simply too large and too influential to ignore.

I will be using much of the data from an excellent book by Thom and Jess Rainer, *The Millennials: Connecting to America's Largest Generation*.[124] The Lifeway survey of 1,200 older Millennials (born between 1980 and 1991) provides a detailed look at this generation.

We should begin by noting that not only are Millennials the largest generation, they are also one of the most diverse. That means that for every trend we identify in this generation, there are also lots of exceptions. But that doesn't mean we can't learn some key facets of the Millennials. Here are just a few characteristics.

First, they are on track to become America's most educated generation. "In 2007, the first year the twenty-five- to twenty-nine-year-old age group was entirely comprised of Millennials, 30 percent had attained a

---

[124] Thom Rainer and Jess Rainer, *The Millennials: Connecting to America's Largest Generation* (Nashville, B&H Publishing Group, 2011).

college degree. That is the highest rate ever recorded for that age group."[125]

Second, Millennials view marriage differently than previous generations. They are marrying later, if at all. The average age for first marriage has increased approximately five years since 1970 for both men and women. "About 65 percent of young adults cohabit at least once prior to marriage, compared to just 10 percent in the 1960s."[126]

Finally, Millennials are the least religious generation in American history. They may say that they are spiritual, but only a small fraction of them says that is important in their lives. The sad reality is that most Millennials don't think about religion at all.

Perhaps the most amazing response from the survey of Millennials was that they are hopeful. Consider their response to the simple statement: "I believe I can do something great." About 60 percent agreed strongly with this statement, and another 36 percent agreed somewhat. That was almost every respondent, 96 percent in total.[127]

Marriage and Family

How does the Millennial generation view marriage and family? One way to answer that question is to look at the characteristics of their parents.

Baby Boomers wanted the best for themselves. They had a level of self-centeredness that eventually shifted toward meeting the needs of their children. They wanted everything to be perfect for the Millennial children.

There was a high level of parental involvement. Hence, the parents of Millennials are often called "helicopter parents." When Millennials were asked about

---

[125] Ibid., 3.
[126] Ibid.
[127] Ibid., 16.

parental involvement, 89 percent responded that they received guidance and advice from their parents.[128] It turns out that the Boomers are helping Millennials make decisions about work and life. Sometimes the parents sit in on job interviews and even try to negotiate salaries. While previous generations might have rejected such advice, 87 percent of Millennials view their parents as a positive source of influence.[129]

This positive view Millennials have of parents extends to the older generation as a whole. While Baby Boomers tended to be antiauthoritarian, Millennials have a very positive attitude towards those who are older. Of the Millennials interviewed, 94 percent said they have great respect for older generations.[130]

When it comes to marriage, Millennials are still optimistic about it even though they grew up in a world where divorce was common. They were asked to respond to the following statement: "It is likely that I will marry more than one time in my life." For those who responded, 86 percent disagreed that they will marry more than once.[131] Apparently, most Millennials plan to marry once or not at all. It is also worth noting that Millennials are marrying much later than any generation that had preceded them.

Millennials also view marriage differently in part because of the political battles concerning same-sex marriage and the definition of marriage. In the survey of Millennials, they were asked to respond to this statement: "I see nothing wrong with two people of the same gender getting married." Six in ten agree with the statement (40 percent strongly agreed, 21 percent agreed

---

[128] Ibid., 55.
[129] Ibid., 56.
[130] Ibid., 59.
[131] Ibid., 63.

somewhat).[132] Put simply, a significant majority of Millennials see nothing wrong with same-sex marriage.

The impact of technology on marriage and family is significant. The Millennial generation has grown up with the Internet, cell phones, and social media. It is easier than ever to call on a cell phone or send a text to other members of one's extended family. Posting pictures on Facebook allow family members to immediately see what is happening to their children and grandchildren. Millennials are introducing their families to a variety of ways to stay connected.

Motivating the Millennials

How can we motivate the Millennial generation? The answer to that question is easy: build relationships. Thom and Jess Rainer put it this way. "The best motivators in the workplace for this generation are relationships. The best connectors in religious institutions are relationships. The best way to get a Millennial involved in a service, activity, or ministry is through relationships."[133]

Relationships are important because of their connection to their family. Millennials also see the world as a much smaller place since they can visit anywhere in the world (either in person or on the Internet). And they are connected to people through the new media in ways that no other generation was able to do.

Education is a high priority for Millennials. This generation is on pace to have significantly more college degrees than the rest of the nation as a whole. About a quarter of the current U.S. population over 25 years old

---

[132] Ibid., 66.
[133] Ibid., 105.

has a college degree, but nearly four in ten of Millennials will probably receive a degree.[134]

Millennials do want to make money, but they are not driven by money. Their motivation for education and career are motivated more by family and friends. One word that often surfaces is the word "flexibility." They see money as a means to do what they want to do. At the same time, they reject the "keeping up with the Jones' mentality" that often drives their parents.

Religion is not much of a motivating factor for Millennials. Spiritual matters are not important to them. Only 13 percent of them viewed religion and spirituality as important. And even among those who described themselves as Christian, only 18 percent said their religion was important to them.[135]

Only one group in the study said their faith was important to them. This was the subgroup identified as "Evangelicals" because of their orthodox biblical beliefs. Nearly two-thirds (65 percent) said their faith was important to them.[136]

The political orientation of Millennials will no doubt influence elections. Millennials voted for Barack Obama over John McCain in the 2008 election by a two-to-one margin (66 percent to 32 percent). It is also worth noting that only half of the Millennials were eligible to vote that year. A greater percentage of that generation will become eligible to vote in each new election cycle.

Various polls, including exit polls, showed that this generation wanted more centralized power in government. And by more than a two-to-one margin (71 percent to 29 percent) they thought the federal government should guarantee health-care coverage for all

---

[134] Ibid., 108.
[135] Ibid., 111.
[136] Ibid., 112.

Americans. More than six out of ten felt that government should be responsible for providing for their retirement.[137]

Millennials and Media

The Millennial generation has been influenced by media and technology like no other generation. Social commentators made much of the influence of television on the Baby Boomers, but the proliferation of Internet, smartphones, and social media has had an even greater impact on Millennials.

When technology first comes on the scene, there are early adopters, then a significant majority, and finally laggards. Millennials fit into the category of early adopters. In the survey they were asked if they agree with the following statement: "I am usually among the first people to acquire products featuring new technology." About half agreed with the statement, and half disagreed with the statement.[138] And even for those who disagreed, it is safe to say they did not fit into the category of laggards. Millennials are quick to embrace new technology.

There is one technology that Millennials always have in their hands: video games. "Video-game consoles are part of the industry that pulled in more than twenty billion dollars in revenue in 2008."[139] If there was one form of technology that is easily identifiable with Millennials, it is video games.

When asked how they most frequently communicate when not actually with the other person, they rated phone first (39 percent), then texting (37

---

[137] Ibid., 115.
[138] Ibid., 188.
[139] Ibid.

percent), and then e-mail (16 percent). At the bottom was by letter (1 percent). The survey also noticed a difference between older and younger Millennials. Put simply, the younger you are, the more likely you are to communicate by texting.

Social media is also a significant part of the lifestyle of a Millennial. Not surprisingly, the most popular social media site is,

- Facebook with 1,100,000,000 - Estimated Unique Monthly Visitors
- YouTube with 1,000,000,000 - Estimated Unique Monthly Visitors
- Twitter with 310,000,000 - Estimated Unique Monthly Visitors
- LinkedIn with 255,000,000 - Estimated Unique Monthly Visitors
- Pinterest with 250,000,000 - Estimated Unique Monthly Visitors
- Google+ with 120,000,000 - Estimated Unique Monthly Visitors
- Tumblr with 110,000,000 - Estimated Unique Monthly Visitors
- Instagram with 100,000,000 - Estimated Unique Monthly Visitors
- Reddit with 85,000,000 - Estimated Unique Monthly Visitors

Although social media can be accessed in many ways, still the most pervasive is through the computer. Millennials use computers both for work and for personal use. Most Millennials (83 percent) use a computer for work and spend about 17 hours on it each week. One out of five Millennials uses their computer for work for

40 or more hours per week.[140] And Millennials spend time on computers for personal use. The responses ranged from 5 hours per week to 30 hours per week. The average was 17 hours per week.

If you put these numbers together, you find something shocking. The average Millennial spends 17 hours per week on a computer for work and spends the same amount of time on a computer for personal use. That totals 34 hours per week on a computer. "That means that roughly one-third of Millennials' waking lives are spent on a computer."[141]

Millennials and Religion

The Millennial generation is the least religious generation in American history. The survey found that they are likely to have a syncretistic belief system. In other words, he or she will take portions of belief from various faiths and non-faiths and blend them together into a unique spiritual system.

Thom and Jess Rainer found that this generation is less likely to care about religion or spiritual matters than previous generations. When they were asked in an open-ended question what was important to them, spiritual matters were sixth on the list. Preceding them in importance were family, friends, education, career, and spouse/partner.

When asked to describe themselves, two-thirds (65 percent) used the term Christian. Interestingly, nearly three in ten (28 percent) picked either atheism, agnosticism, or no preference. In other words, they have moved completely away from certain belief in God.

---

[140] Ibid., 197.
[141] Ibid., 197.

When asked if they were "born-again Christians", using a precise definition provided by the interviewers, only 20 percent affirmed this definition of belief and experience. And when presented with seven statements about orthodox Christian belief, the researchers found that only 6 percent of Millennials could affirm them and thus could be properly defined as Evangelical.[142]

A third (34 percent) of Millennials said that no one can know what will happen when they die. But more than one-fourth (26 percent) said they believe they will go to heaven when they die because they have accepted Christ as their Savior.[143]

Church attendance has been decreasing with each generation. The Millennial generation illustrates that trend. Nearly two-thirds (65 percent) rarely or never attend religious services.[144] About one-fourth (24 percent) are active in church (meaning they attend at least once a week). This might suggest that a number of Millennials who attend church do so as seekers. In other words, they are at least spiritually interested enough to visit a church even though they may not be saved.

The Millennial generation presents a significant challenge for us as Christians. The largest and least religious generation in American history is here and making an impact. If the church and Christian organizations are to be vibrant and effective in the twenty-first century, pastors and Christian leaders need to know how to connect to the Millennials. The first step is understanding them and their beliefs. That is why I recommend the book by Thom and Jess Rainer and encourage you to get other information on this generation.

---

[142] Ibid., 232.
[143] Ibid., 233.
[144] Ibid., 236.

CHAPTER 14 Sex and Violence on Television

Is there too much sex and violence on television? Most Americans seem to think so. One survey found that seventy-five percent of Americans felt that television had "too much sexually explicit material." Moreover, eighty-six percent believed that television had contributed to "a decline in values."[145] Channel surfing through the television reveals plots celebrating premarital sex, adultery, and even homosexuality.

The Extent of the Problem

Sexual promiscuity in the media appears to be at an all-time high. A study of adolescents (ages twelve to seventeen) showed that watching sex on TV influences teens to have sex. Youths were more likely to initiate intercourse as well as other sexual activities.[146]

A study by the Parents Television Council found that prime time network television is more violent than ever before. In addition, they found that this increasing violence is also of a sexual nature. They found that portrayals of violence are up seventy-five percent since 1998.[147]

The study also provided expert commentary by Deborah Fisher, Ph.D. She states that children, on

---

[145] National Family Values: A Survey of Adults conducted by Voter/Consumer Research (Bethesda, MD, 1994).

[146] Rebecca Collins, et. al., "Watching Sex on Television Predicts Adolescent Initiation of Sexual Behavior," *Pediatrics*, Vol. 114 (3), September 2004.

[147] Kristen Fyfe, "More Violence, More Sex, More Troubled Kids," *Culture and Media Institute*, 11 January 2007, www.cultureandmediainstitute.org.

average, will be exposed to a thousand murders, rapes, and assaults per year through television. She goes on to warn that early exposure to television violence has "consistently emerged as a significant predictor of later aggression."[148]

A previous study by the Parents Television Council compared the changes in sex, language, and violence between decades. The special report entitled *What a Difference a Decade Makes* found many shocking things.[149]

> The data showed that eight of the nine dramas NBC has on air or is soon to debut – all of which are rated TV-14 – contain what the group considers graphic violence and gore, at what it says are unprecedented levels. NBC's three returning dramas, "Revolution," "Chicago Fire" and "Law & Order: SVU," together had far more scenes of violence this season than last season, with violent scenes in "Law & Order: SVU" more than doubling from 10 to 24 scenes of violence this year.
>
> During the past several seasons, networks have taken advantage of their free rein to release a barrage of violent shows – many of them to astounding success. AMC's "The Walking Dead," about a violent, post-apocalyptic zombie wasteland, has set several ratings records, including this Sunday when it opened its fourth season with 16.1 million same-day viewers, a series best. "Breaking Bad," a crime drama centering on a chemistry teacher-turned-meth maker, drew 10.3 million viewers in its series finale, the show's biggest

---

[148] Ibid.

[149] Parents Television Council, Special Report: What a Difference a Decade Makes, 30 March 2000, www.parentstv.org.

showing ever. Repeat murderers also seem to be in vogue: Showtime's "Dexter," about a serial killer, CBS' "Criminal Minds," which profiles criminals, including serial killers, and Fox's"The Following," about an FBI agent chasing a serial killer, have all been hits.[150]

On this, Edward D. Andrews writes,

Parents, teachers, coaches and the like influenced the youth of the 1950s and 1960s. Most young people today are very much influenced by hip-hop, rap, and heavy metal music, as well reality television, celebrities, movies, video games, and the internet, especially social media. Parents are now allowing their children to receive life-altering opinions, beliefs, and worldviews from the likes of Snooki, a cast member of the MTV reality show *Jersey Shore*. Kim Kardashian and her family rose to prominence with their reality television series, *Keeping Up with the Kardashians*.

The ABC Family Channel (owned by Disney) comes across as a channel that you would want you children watching. However, most of the shows are nothing more than dysfunctional families, promotions of homosexuality as an alternative lifestyle, and young actors and actresses that are playing underage teens in high school, running around killing, causing havoc, and having sexual intercourse with multiple characters on the

---

[150] US News & World Report: STUDY: Violence Increasing in TV Dramas — Especially on NBC,

http://www.usnews.com/news/articles/2013/10/18/study-violence-increasing-in-tv-dramas--especially-on-nbc (accessed November 09, 2016).

show. In August 2006, an all-new slogan and visual style premiered on ABC Family: A New Kind of Family. The channel shows such programming as Pretty Little Liars, Twisted, The Fosters, Melissa & Joey, Switched at Birth, The Lying Game, Bunheads and Baby Daddy.

The world has added new words to their vocabulary, like "sexting," which is the act of sending sexually explicit messages and/or photographs, primarily between cell phones. The term was first popularized in 2007. Then, there is the "F-Bomb," which we are not going to define fully other than to say that the dictionary considers it "a lighthearted and printable euphemism" for something far more offensive. If all of the above is unfamiliar to you as a parent, and you have a teen or preteen child, you may want to Google the information.[151]

First, on a per-hour basis, sexual material more than tripled in the last decade. For example, while references to homosexuality were once rare, now they are mainstream. Second, the study found that foul language increased five-fold in just a decade. They also found that the intensity of violent incidents significantly increased.

These studies provide the best quantifiable measure of what has been taking place on television. No longer can defenders of television say that TV is "not that bad." The evidence is in, and television is more offensive than ever.

---

[151] Edward D. Andrews, *For As I Think – In My Heart – So I Am: Combining Biblical Counseling with Cognitive Behavioral Therapy [Second Edition]* (Cambridge, OH: Christian Publishing House, 2016), 238-239.

Christians should not be surprised by these findings. Sex and violence have always been part of the human condition because of our sin nature (Romans 3:23), but modern families are exposed to a level of sex and violence that is unprecedented. Obviously, this will have a detrimental effect. The Bible teaches that "as a man thinks in his heart, so is he" (Proverbs 23:7, KJV). What we see and hear affect our actions. And while this is true for adults, it is especially true for children.

Television's Impact on Behavior

What is the impact of watching television on subsequent behavior? There are abundant studies which document that what you see, hear, and read does affect your perception of the world and your behavior.

The American Academy of Pediatrics in 2000 issued a "Joint Statement on the Impact of Entertainment Violence on Children." They cited over one thousand studies, including reports from the Surgeon General's office and the National Institute of Mental Health. They say that these studies "point overwhelmingly to a causal connection between media violence and aggressive behavior in some children."[152]

In 1992, the American Psychological Association concluded that forty years of research on the link between TV violence and real-life violence has been ignored, stating that "the 'scientific debate is over' and calling for federal policy to protect society."[153]

A 1995 poll of children ten to sixteen years of age showed that children recognize that "what they see on

---

[152] Joint Statement on the Impact of Entertainment Violence on Children, *American Academy of Pediatrics*, 26 July 2000.

[153] David Grossman, "What the Surgeon General Found; As Early as 1972, the Link Was Clear Between Violent TV and Movies and Violent Youths," *Los Angeles Times*, 21 October 1999, B-11.

television encourages them to take part in sexual activity too soon, to show disrespect for their parents, [and] to lie and to engage in aggressive behavior." More than two-thirds said they are influenced by television; seventy-seven percent said TV shows too much sex before marriage, and sixty-two percent said sex on television and in movies influences their peers to have sexual relations when they are too young. Two-thirds also cited certain programs featuring dysfunctional families as encouraging disrespect toward parents.

The report reminds us that television sets the baseline standard for the entire entertainment industry. Most homes (ninety-eight percent) have a television set. And according to recent statistics, that TV in the average household is on more than eight hours each day.[154]

By contrast, other forms of entertainment (such as movies, DVDs, CDs) must be sought out and purchased. Television is universally available and thus has the most profound effect on our culture.

As Christians we need to be aware of the impact television has on our families and us. The studies show us that sex and violence on TV can affect us in subtle yet profound ways. We can no longer ignore the growing body of data that suggests that televised imagery does affect our perceptions and behaviors. So we should be concerned about the impact television (as well as other forms of media) has on our neighbors and our society as a whole.

Sex on Television

Most Americans believe there is too much sex on television. A survey conducted in 1994 found that

---

[154] "Average home has more TVs than people," *USA Today*, 21 September 2006, www.usatoday.com/life/television/news/2006-09-21-homes-tv_x.htm

seventy-five percent of Americans felt that television had "too much sexually explicit material." Moreover, eighty-six percent believed that television had contributed to "a decline in values."[155] As we documented earlier, sexual promiscuity on television is at an all-time high.

Many studies on pornography illustrate the dangerous effects of sex, especially when linked with violence.[156] Neil Malamuth and Edward Donnerstein document the volatile impact of sex and violence in the media. They say, "There can be relatively long-term, antisocial effects of movies that portray sexual violence as having positive consequences."[157]

In a message given by Donnerstein, he concluded with this warning and observation: "If you take normal males and expose them to graphic violence against women in R-rated films, the research doesn't show that they'll commit acts of violence against women. It doesn't say they will go out and commit rape. But it does demonstrate that they become less sensitized to violence against women, they have less sympathy for rape victims, and their perceptions and attitudes and values about violence change."[158]

It is important to remember that these studies are applicable not just to hard-core pornography. Many of the studies used films that are readily shown on television (especially cable television) any night of the week. And

---

[155] National Family Values: A Survey of Adults conducted by Voter/Consumer Research (Bethesda, MD, 1994).

[156] . Kerby Anderson, "The Pornography Plague," Probe Ministries, 1997, www.probe.org/pornography/.

[157] Neil Malamuth and Edward Donnerstein, *Pornography and Sexual Aggression* (New York: Academic, 1984).

[158] Edward Donnerstein, "What the Experts Say," a forum at the Industry-wide Leadership Conference on Violence in Television Programming, 2 August 1993, in *National Council for Families and Television Report*, 9.

many of the movies shown today in theaters are much more explicit than those shown just a few years ago.

Social commentator Irving Kristol asked this question in a *Wall Street Journal* column: "Can anyone really believe that soft porn in our Hollywood movies, hard porn in our cable movies and violent porn in our 'rap' music is without effect? Here the average, overall impact is quite discernible to the naked eye. And at the margin, the effects, in terms most notably of illegitimacy and rape, are shockingly visible."[159]

Christians must be careful that sexual images on television don't conform us to the world (Rom. 12:2). Instead, we should use discernment. Philippians 4:8 says, "Finally, brothers, whatever is true, whatever is noble, whatever is right, whatever is pure, whatever is lovely, whatever is admirable if anything is excellent or praiseworthy, think about such things."

Sex on television is at an all-time high, so we should be even more careful to screen what our families and we see. Christians should be concerned about the images we see on television.

Violence on Television

Children's greatest exposure to violence comes from television. TV shows, movies edited for television, and video games expose young children to a level of violence unimaginable just a few years ago. The American Psychological Association says the average child watches eight thousand televised murders and one hundred thousand acts of violence before finishing elementary

---

[159] Irving Kristol, "Sex, Violence and Videotape," *Wall Street Journal*, 31 May 1994.

school.[160] That number more than doubles by the time he or she reaches age eighteen.

At a very young age, children see a level of graphic violence and mayhem that in the past may have been seen only by a few police officers and military personnel. TV brings hitting, kicking, stabbings, shootings, and dismemberment right into homes on a daily basis.

The impact on behavior is predictable. Two prominent Surgeon General reports in the last two decades link violence on television and aggressive behavior in children and teenagers. In addition, the National Institute of Mental Health issued a ninety-four-page report, *Television, and Behavior: Ten Years of Scientific Progress and Implications for the Eighties.* They found "overwhelming" scientific evidence that "excessive" violence on television spills over into the playground and the streets.[161] In one five-year study of 732 children, "several kinds of aggression, conflicts with parents, fighting, and delinquency, were all positively correlated with the total amount of television viewing."[162]

Long-term studies are even more disturbing. University of Illinois psychologist Leonard Eron studied children at age eight and then again at eighteen. He found that television habits established at the age of eight influenced aggressive behavior throughout childhood and adolescent years. The more violent the programs preferred by boys in the third grade, the more aggressive their behavior, both at that time and ten years later. He,

---

[160] John Johnston, "Kids: Growing Up Scared," *Cincinnati Enquirer*, March 20, 1994, p. E01.

[161] Cited in "Warning from Washington," *Time*, 17 May 1982, 77.

[162] James Mann, "What Is TV Doing to America?" *U.S. News and World Report*, 2 August 1982, 27.

therefore, concluded that "the effect of television violence on aggression is cumulative."[163]

Twenty years later Eron and Rowell Huesmann found the pattern continued. He and his researchers found that children who watched significant amounts of TV violence at the age of eight were consistently more likely to commit violent crimes or engage in child or spouse abuse at thirty.[164] They concluded that: "heavy exposure to televised violence is one of the causes of aggressive behavior, crime and violence in society. Television violence affects youngsters of all ages, of both genders, at all socioeconomic levels and all levels of intelligence."[165]

Violent images on television affect children in adverse ways and Christians should be concerned about the impact.

Biblical Perspective

Television is such a part of our lives that we often are unaware of its subtle and insidious influence. Nearly every home has a television set, so we tend to take it for granted and are often oblivious to its influence.

I've had many people tell me that they watch television and that it has no impact at all on their worldview or behavior. However, the Bible teaches that "as a man thinks in his heart, so is he" (Proverbs 23:7). What we view and what we think about affects our actions. And there is abundant psychological evidence that television viewing affects our worldview.

---

[163] Leo Bogart, "Warning: The Surgeon General Has Determined that TV Violence Is Moderately Dangerous to Your Child's Mental Health," *Public Opinion* (Winter, 1972-73): 504.

[164] Peter Plagen, "Violence in Our Culture," *Newsweek*, 1 April 1991, 51.

[165] Ibid.

George Gerbner and Larry Gross, working at the Annenberg School of Communications in the 1970s, found that heavy television viewers live in a scary world. "We have found that people who watch a lot of TV see the real world as more dangerous and frightening than those who watch very little. Heavy viewers are less trustful of their fellow citizens, and more fearful of the real world."[166] Heavy viewers also tended to overestimate their likelihood of being involved in a violent crime. They defined heavy viewers as those adults who watch an average of four or more hours of television a day. Approximately one-third of all American adults fit that category.

If this is true of adults, imagine how television violence affects children's perceptions of the world. Gerbner and Gross say, "Imagine spending six hours a day at the local movie house when you were twelve years old. No parent would have permitted it. Yet, in our sample of children, nearly half of the twelve-year-olds watch an average of six or more hours of television per day." This would mean that a large portion of young people fit into the category of heavy viewers. Television profoundly shapes their view of the world. Gerbner and Gross, therefore, conclude: "If adults can be so accepting of the reality of television, imagine its effect on children. By the time the average American child reaches public school, he has already spent several years in an electronic nursery school."[167]

Television viewing affects both adults and children in subtle ways. We must not ignore the growing body of data that suggests that televised imagery does affect our perceptions and behaviors. Our worldview and our subsequent actions are affected by what we see on

---

[166] George Gerbner and Larry Gross, "The Scary World of TV's Heavy Viewer," *Psychology Today*, April 1976.
[167] Ibid.

television. Christians, therefore, must be careful not to let television conform us to the world (Romans 12:2), but instead should develop a Christian worldview.

CHAPTER 15 Kids Killing Kids

Not so long ago the biggest problem kids faced was getting a flat tire on their bikes or having a mean teacher assign homework over the weekend. How times have changed. Who would have guessed that one of the perennial stories would be kids killing kids?

In this chapter, we're going to talk about the issue of school shootings and the broader issue of kids killing kids. Why is this happening? What can be done to stem the tide of violence on campus and society? We'll look at such topics as video games, teenage rebellion, and tolerance. And we'll also look at the spiritual aspects as well.

Each time we hear about gunshots on a high school campus we are once again reminded that we are living in a different world. The body count of students and teachers causes us to shake our heads and wonder what is going on. In some cases, the shooters are teenagers with elaborate plans and evil desires. But sometimes the hail of bullets comes from impulsive kids as young as eleven years old.

In the past, when we did talk about kids killing kids, it was in an urban setting. Gangland battles between the Bloods and the Crips reminded us that life in the inner city was hard and ruthless. But the latest battlegrounds have not been Watts, the Bronx, or Cabrini-Green. These violent confrontations have taken place in rural, idyllic towns with names like Pearl, Mississippi and Paducah, Kentucky and Sandy Hook, Connecticut and Jonesboro, Arkansas and Littleton, Colorado.

We are shocked and surprised. We open our newspapers to see the faces of kids caught up in the occult, and we wonder how they were attracted to such evil. We open those newspapers again, and we see the faces of Opie and Beaver look-alikes charged with five counts of murder and we wonder if they even understood what they were doing.

The answers from pundits have been many. Young people are desensitized to violence, and they learn to kill by using point-and-shoot video games. Teenagers are rebellious, and they are looking for a way to defy authority. In the past, that was easier to accomplish by merely violating the dress code. Today, in a society that values tolerance, trying to come up with a behavior that is shocking is getting harder and harder to do. And the social and spiritual climate that our kids live in is hardly conducive to moral living.

Kids killing kids, I believe, is the best evidence yet of a culture in chaos that has turned its back on God's moral law. Do we really believe that children can see thousands of TV murders or play violent computer games and not be tempted to act out that violence in real life? Do we think we can lower societal standards and not have kids act out in very bizarre ways? Do we think we can pull God from the schools and prayer from the classroom and see no difference in the behavior of children? We shouldn't be surprised. Kids killing kids is evidence of a nation in moral free fall.

The Media and Video Games

What is the influence of the media and video games? We shouldn't be surprised that there is empirical evidence that it is having an effect on our kids.

One person who knows about this is Lt. Col. Dave Grossman. He is a retired West Point psychology professor, Army Ranger, and an expert in the study of violence in war and killing. He is also an instructor at Arkansas State University in Jonesboro and was one of the first on the scene of the Jonesboro, Arkansas shootings. He has a lot to say.

He saw the devastation wrought by the shootings—not just the five dead and ten wounded. He saw what happens when violence intrudes into everyday life. And, where he's been, he sees where the violence comes from. He says, "Anywhere television appears, fifteen years later, the murder rate doubles."[168]

He says, "In the video games, in the movies, on the television, the one behavior that is consistently depicted in glamorous terms and consistently rewarded is killing." He believes that media violence was a significant factor in the killings in Pearl, Mississippi, in West Paducah, Kentucky, in Jonesboro, Arkansas, in Springfield, Oregon, and in Littleton, Colorado.

He also says that the combination of a sense of inferiority and the exposure to violence can provoke violence in young boys who are "wannabes." Sometimes they see violence as a route to fame, and one has to wonder whether all the media exposure of these school shootings will spawn even more.

Consider the 1995 movie, *The Basketball Diaries*. In the film, Leonardo DiCaprio (also of *Titanic* fame) goes into a schoolroom and shoots numerous children and teachers. In doing so, he became a role model for young boys who are "wannabes."

The parents of three students killed in Paducah, Kentucky have brought a lawsuit against the company that distributed the film *The Basketball Diaries*. The parents' lawyer points out that Michael Carneal, who opened fire on a group of students in Kentucky, viewed the film and honed his shooting skills by playing computer games such as *Doom* and *Redneck Rampage*.

---

[168] Andrea Billups and Jerry Seper, "Experts Hit Permissiveness in Schools, Violence on TV," *The Washington Times*, 22 April 1999.

Dave Grossman goes into some detail in showing how violence in films, videos, and television can affect us. The parallels in his book *On Killing: The Psychological Cost of Learning to Kill in War and Society*[169] and what is happening in the media today are chilling. Two factors are desensitization and operant conditioning. Show soldiers (or children) enough visual images of violence, and they will become desensitized to it. Practice shooting targets of people and conditioning will eventually take over. In some ways, it doesn't matter whether it's soldiers doing target practice at a range or kids using point-and-shoot video games. The chilling result is the same: the creation of a killing machine.

You don't need to read Grossman's book to see the parallels. Young people today are exposed to violent images that desensitize them and make it possible for some to act out these violent images in real life. And video games help them hone their shooting skills and overcome their hesitation to kill. Dave Grossman has seen it in war, and now he sees it in everyday life.

Violence and Teenage Rebellion

So many words have been spoken in the last few months about school shootings that it's often difficult to hear sound commentary in the midst of the cacophony. But one voice that deserves a hearing is Jonathan Cohen who wrote a commentary in the *New York Post* entitled "Defining Rebellion Up."[170]

Years ago Senator Daniel Patrick Moynihan wrote a seminal piece in an academic journal entitled "Defining

---

[169] Dave Grossman, *On Killing: The Psychological Cost of Learning to Kill in War and Society* (New York: Little, Brown, 1996).

[170] Jonathan Cohen, "Defining Rebellion Up," *New York Post*, 27 April 1999.

Deviancy Down."[171] It was his contention that in the midst of cultural chaos we tend to redefine what is normal. When the crime rate goes through the roof, we say that crime is inevitable in a free society. When the illegitimate birth rate quadruples, we say that maybe two parents in a home aren't really necessary after all. In essence, what society has done is follow the pattern in Isaiah 5:20 of calling evil good and good evil.

Jonathan Cohen picks up on that theme and extends it to our current crisis. He says that when America became willing to define deviancy down, it simultaneously defined rebellion up. He says, "Anti-social teens are nothing new, but as deviancy has been made normal, we have made it increasingly difficult for teenagers to rebel."

Adults are no longer offended or outraged by behavior that would have sent our parents through the roof. Unfortunately, we have learned the lessons of tolerance well. We tolerate just about everything from tattoos to black nail polish to metal pierced eyebrows.

Jonathan Cohen says, "We have raised the threshold of rebellion so high that it is practically beyond reach. To be recognized, to get attention, to stir anyone in authority to lift a finger, whether it is a parent, a teacher, a principal, or a sheriff, a rebel has to go to very great lengths these days. One must send letter bombs, blow up office buildings or gun down children."

If a young person is trying to defy authority, it does take quite a bit to be recognized. Just a few decades ago, when dress codes were still in effect, a student could be somewhat rebellious without getting into too much trouble or hurting other people. Today, it apparently takes quite a bit to run afoul of those in authority.

---

[171] Daniel Patrick Moynihan, "Defining Deviancy Down," *The American Spectator*, Winter 1993.

Jonathan Cohen asks, "And what of the teachers at Columbine High? It seemed they were not disturbed at all by the boys' odd conduct. In fact, one instructor actually helped them make a video dramatizing their death-and-destruction fantasy. For all we know, he may well have commended himself for being so nonjudgmental."

This surfaces an important issue. The highest value in our society today has become tolerance. We are not to judge others. When you put this trend of rising rebellion with increased tolerance together, you end up with a lethal mixture.

Jonathan Cohen concludes by wondering if all of this might have been different. He says, "If teachers had forbidden their students from coming to class wearing black trenchcoats, fingernail polish, and makeup, Littleton likely would not be a name on everyone's lips. If the principal had had the common sense to ban a group of boys from coming to school sporting Nazi regalia, marching through the corridors in military fashion and calling themselves the Trench Coat Mafia, Columbine High School might not be behind a police line."

Tolerance

Tolerance has become the highest value in our society today, and I believe that it may explain why we miss the signals that something is wrong with our kids.

After the school shooting in Colorado, an editorial appeared in the *New York Post*.[172] The editorial writers said, "The Littleton massacre could prove a turning point in American society—one of those moments when the entire culture changes course."

---

[172] "Too Much Tolerance?" *New York Post*, 27 April 1999.

Apparently, it was not a turning point. Nevertheless, the editorial writers made a strong case that one of the things that must change is our contemporary view of tolerance.

The editorial was entitled "Too Much Tolerance?" While other pundits focused on guns, video games, and other cultural phenomena, these editorial writers said the real cause was "inattention."

After all, the killers in Colorado were sending out signals of an impending calamity. It's just that no one was paying attention. For example, one Littleton parent went to the police twice about threats made on his son's life by Eric Harris. His pleas were to no avail. The cops didn't pay attention.

These kids in the Trench Coat Mafia gave each other Hitler salutes at a local bowling alley. But the community didn't pay attention.

These same kids marched down the hallways and got into fights with jocks and other kids after school. But the school didn't pay attention.

One kid's mother works with disabled kids, but seemed unaware that her own son had a fascination with Adolf Hitler and spent a year planning the destruction of the high school.

Again parents didn't pay attention.

Throughout the article, the editorial writers recount all the things these kids did. They conclude that while they "were doing everything they could to offend the community they lived in, the community chose to pay them no heed."

Why? I believe that this tragic lack of attention is the sorry harvest of tolerance and diversity preached in the nation's classrooms every day. We are not to judge others. The only sin in society is the sin of judgmentalism.

We cannot judge hairstyles or lifestyles, manners or morals. We may think another person's dress, actions, or lifestyles are a bit different, but we are told not to judge. Everything must be tolerated. And so we decide to ignore in the name of tolerance. In essence, inattention is the fruit of a message of tolerance and diversity.

In decades past, boundaries existed, school dress codes were enforced, and certain behavior was not allowed. As the boundaries were dropped and the lines blurred, teachers and parents learned to cope by paying less attention.

The editorial writers, therefore, conclude (and please excuse the bluntness of their statement) that, "The only way Americans can live like this is to tune out, to ignore, to refuse to pay attention. In the name of broad-mindedness, Littleton allowed Harris and Klebold to fall through the cracks straight to Hell."

So why do we have kids killing kids? There are lots of reasons: the moral breakdown of society, video games, rebellion. But another reason is tolerance. We have been taught for decades not to judge, and this has given adults a license to be inattentive.

Spiritual Issues

Let's look at some spiritual issues associated with so many of these school shootings.

Perhaps the best way to begin is to quote former Education Secretary Bill Bennett. He was on one of the talking-head shows discussing the tragedy in Littleton, Colorado. All of a sudden he turned directly to the television camera and said, "Hello?"

That was the attention-getter. But what he said afterward should also get our attention. He pointed out that these kids were walking the halls in trench coats, and apparently that didn't really get the attention of the teachers and administrators. But, he said if a kid walked the halls with a Bible, now that would probably get their attention. Something is very wrong with a society and a school system that would admonish a school kid for carrying a Bible and spreading the good news while ignoring a group of kids wearing trench coats and spreading hate.

In her *Wall Street Journal* column former presidential speechwriter Peggy Noonan talked about "The Culture of Death" our children live in.[173] She quoted headlines from news stories, and frankly I can't even repeat what she quoted. Our kids are up to their necks in really awful stuff, and it comes to them day after day on television, in the movies, and in the newspapers.

She then asked, Who counters this culture of death? Well, parents do, and churches do. But they aren't really given much of a place in our society today. In fact, Peggy Noonan told a story to illustrate her point.

She said, "A man called into Christian radio this morning and said a true thing. He said, and I am paraphrasing: Those kids were sick and sad, and if a teacher had talked to one of them and said, 'Listen, there's a way out, there really is love out there that will never stop loving you, there's a real God, and I want to be able to talk to you about him'—if that teacher had intervened that way, he would have been hauled into court."

You know that man who called that radio station is right. A few years ago, a very famous case made its way through the Colorado courts. A high school teacher in Colorado was taken to court merely because he had a Bible on his desk. If you haven't heard the story, I guess

---

[173] Peggy Noonan, "The Culture of Death," Wall Street Journal, 22 April 1999.

the conclusion wouldn't surprise you. The teacher lost the case and lost it again on appeal.

As we've talked about the disturbing phenomenon of kids killing kids, we have discussed the breakdown of society, video games, rebellion, and tolerance. But we shouldn't forget the spiritual dimension. We are reaping the harvest of a secular society.

Kids kill other kids, and so we wonder why. We throw God out of the classroom, we throw the Bible out of the classroom, we throw prayer out of the classroom, and we even throw the Ten Commandments out of the classroom.

Maybe we shouldn't wonder why any longer. Maybe we should be surprised the society isn't more barbaric given the fact that so many positive, spiritual influences have been thrown out. The ultimate solution to the problem of kids killing kids is for the nation to return to God.

CHAPTER 16 Video Games

Grand Theft Auto

One of the best-selling video games in America was "Grand Theft Auto: San Andreas." The controversy over this popular video game is just another reminder of the deception of ratings and the need for parental direction and discernment when it comes to buying video games.

The game in question already has a bad reputation. The National Institute on Media and the Family described it this way: "Raunchy, violent and portraying just about every deviant act that a criminal could think of in full, living 3D graphics. Grand Theft Auto takes the cake again as one of the year's worst games for kids. The premise—restore respect to your neighborhood as you take on equally corrupt San Andreas police."[174]

Ironically, what caused the controversy over the game was not its overt violence and sexuality. What caused a national stir was what was hidden within the game. Those playing the game (known as gamers) could download a modification of "Grand Theft Auto" that would allow them to see graphic sex scenes on screen.

Initially, the distributor distanced itself from what hackers could do with their product once it was on the market. But that argument fell flat when it was found that the downloaded modification merely unlocked pornographic material already within the game. It now turns out that skilled players can unlock the pornographic content without downloading the key from the Internet. The game initially had a "Mature" rating. The Entertainment Software Ratings Board now requires that it be labeled "Adults Only."

---

[174] National Institute on Media and the Family, "Expanded Game Reviews," www.mediafamily.org/kidscore/games_gta4.shtml

"Grand Theft Auto" has already been a lightning rod for controversy because it rewards players for committing crimes and engaging in dangerous and immoral behavior. Gamers can buy and sell drugs, steal cars, run down pedestrians, even feed people into a wood chipper. Nevertheless, the game has sold more than five million copies in the United States.

Who is buying this game? Some are adults buying the game for themselves, but a large percentage of the people buying this game are parents or grandparents buying the game for their kids or grandkids.

Columnist Mona Charen points out that the original concerns about this game surfaced when a Manhattan grandmother bought the game for her fourteen-year-old grandson. Then she was shocked to find out that he could modify the game by downloading material from the Internet. Charen asks, "So, a kindly eighty-five-year-old lady has no qualms about purchasing a gang-glorifying, violence-soaked, sick entertainment for her teenage grandson, but is shocked when it turns out to contain explicit sex? Wasn't the rest enough?"[175]

In most cases, parents and grandparents are buying these games and need to exercise discernment. Many games are harmless and even can help stimulate the mind. Some are questionable. And others are violent and sexually explicit. We need to use discernment in selecting these games.

Benefits of Video Games

A recent article in *Discover* magazine talked about the perception most people have of video game players. It said this is "the classic stereotype of gamers as

---

[175] Mona Charen, "Grand Theft Auto and us," 5 August 2005, www.townhall.com/columnists/monacharen/mc20050805.shtml

attention-deficit-crazed stimulus junkies, easily distracted by flashy graphics and on-screen carnage."[176] Yet new research shows that gaming can be mentally enriching with such cognitive benefits as: pattern recognition, system thinking, and even patience.[177]

One of the best-known studies (done by Shawn Green and Daphne Bavelier) found that playing an action video game markedly improved performance on a range of visual skills related to detecting objects in briefly flashed displays. They found that gamers exhibit superior performance relative to non-gamers on a set of benchmark visual tasks.[178]

What they found was the action video gamers tend to be more attuned to their surroundings. While this occurs while performing within the video game, it also transfers to such things as driving down a residential street where they are more likely than a non-gamer to pick out a child running into the street after a ball.

They found that gamers can process visual information more quickly and can track 30 percent more objects than non-gamers. These conclusions came from testing both gamers and non-gamers with a series of three tests.

The first test flashed a small object on a screen for 1/160 of a second, and the participant would indicate where it flashed. Gamers tended to notice the object far more often than non-gamers.

The second test flashed a number of small objects on a screen at once. The subjects had to type the number of

---

[176] Steven Johnson, "Your Brain on Video Games," *Discover*, July 2005, 40.
[177] Ibid.
[178] C. Shawn Green and Daphne Bavelier, "Action video game modifies visual selective attention," *Nature* 423 (2003), 534-537.

objects they saw. Gamers saw the correct number more often than non-gamers.

The third test flashed black letters and one white letter on a screen in fast succession. The one white letter was sometimes followed by a black "X." Gamers were able to pick out the white letter more often than non-gamers and could more accurately say whether it was followed by a black "X."

The researchers also wanted to know whether the superior performance of gamers was acquired or self-selected. In other words, do video games actually improve visual attention skills or is it possible that visually attentive people choose to play video games?

Green and Bavelier trained a selection of non-gamers on one of two video games. One group played the World War II action video game "Medal of Honor." The other group served as the control group and played the puzzle game "Tetris." The researchers found that after two weeks, the group trained on the World War II game showed a marked increase in performance over the control group.

The researchers, therefore, concluded: "By forcing players to simultaneously juggle a number of varied tasks (detect new enemies, track existing enemies and avoid getting hurt, among others), action-video-game playing pushed the limits of three rather different aspects of visual attention."[179]

Video games can also train our brain to be more efficient. In the early 1990s, Richard Haier (University of California at Irving's Department of Psychiatry and Human Behavior), scanned the brains of "Tetris" players. He found that in first-time users, the brain requires lots of energy. In fact, cerebral glucose metabolic rates actually soar. But after a few weeks, these rates sink to normal as

---

[179] Ibid., 536.

performance increases seven-fold.[180] In essence, "Tetris" trains your brain to stop using inefficient gray matter.

Types of Video Games

Let's now focus on the rating of video games and the major video game categories. As we mentioned earlier, the video game industry is self-regulated, so we need to exercise discernment.

EC – Early Childhood (age 3 and older) – These games are appropriate for anyone who can play a video game and contains no inappropriate material.

E – Everyone (age 6 and older) – These games are designed for younger players and are the equivalent of a PG movie.

T – Teen (age 13 and older) – Generally these games are not appropriate for younger ages and are equivalent of a PG-13 movie.

M – Mature (age 17 and older) – These games are not appropriate for children. They may be rated as such because of overt violence, sexual content, and profanity.

AO – Adults Only (ages 18 and older) – These games involve excessive violence, sexual content, and explicit language.

There are a number of different types of video games.

Puzzles – Puzzle games are usually acceptable for all ages and generally are rated "E." These games involve logic and spatial arrangements. The best-known puzzle game is "Tetris."

---

[180] Jeffrey Goldsmith, "This is Your Brain on Tetris," *Wired*, Issue 2.05, May 1994, 2.

Strategy – These games may be as straightforward as "Chessmaster" or involve the use of tactical moves of troops or players such as "Advanced Wars."

Simulation games – Some games like "SimCity" require creativity and advanced problem-solving skills. Others involve driving or flying simulations that can be relatively tame or highly offensive such as the "Grand Theft Auto" series of video games.

Arcade games – The classic arcade games include such favorites as "Pacman" or "Frogger." However, the newer arcade games may include games like the violent "Street Fighter."

Role playing games – This is a type of game where players assume the roles of via role-playing. Although these games may be less graphic, they often involve fantasy and even the occult.

Action games – These games most often have an "M" rating. Many of these action games involve point-and-shoot games that are especially dangerous.

Violent Video Games

There is cause for concern about violent video games. According to the American Academy of Pediatrics, playing violent video games increases the likelihood of adolescent violent behavior by as much as 13 percent to 22 percent.[181]

A 2005 meta-analysis of over thirty-five research studies (that included 4000 participants) found that "playing violent video games significantly increases physiological arousal and feelings of anger or hostility, and significantly decreases pro-social helping

---

[181] Lori O'Keefe, "Media Exposure Feeding Children's Violent Acts," *American Academy of Pediatrics News*, January 2002.

behavior."[182] Another study has shown a relationship between playing violent video games and being involved in violent acts.[183]

Testimony before the United States Senate documents the following: (1) that violent video games increase violent adolescent behavior, (2) that heavy game players become desensitized to aggression and violence, (3) that nearly 90 percent of all African-American females in these games are victims of violence, and (4) that the most common role for women in violent video games is as prostitutes.[184]

One of the people speaking out against violent video games is Lt. Col. Dave Grossman, whom I have interviewed on a number of occasions. He is a former West Point professor and has written books on the subject of killing.[185] He has also testified that these violent video games are essentially "killing simulators."

Grossman testified on the shooting in Paducah, Kentucky. Michael Carneal, a fourteen-year-old boy who had never fired a handgun before, stole a pistol and fired a few practice shots the night before. The next morning he fired eight shots and had eight hits (four of them head

---

[182] Henry J. Kaiser Family Foundation, "Generation M: Media in the Lives of 8-18 Year Olds," *A Kaiser Family Foundation Study*, March 2005.

[183] Jeanne B. Funk, et. al. "An Evidence-Based Approach to Examining the Impact of Playing Violent Video and Computer Games," *Studies in Media and Information Literacy Education*, Vol. 2, Issue 4 (November 2002), University of Toronto Press.

[184] Craig Anderson, "Violent Video Games Increase Aggression and Violence," U.S. Senate Testimony, Hearing on The Impact of Interactive Violence on Children, Committee on Commerce, Science and Transportation, 106th Congress, 1st Session.

[185] David Grossman, *On Killing: The Psychological Cost of Learning to Kill in War and Society* (New York: Little, Brown and Co, 1995) and David Grossman and G. DeGaetano, *Stop Teaching Our Kids to Kill: A Call to Action Against TV, Movie and Video Game Violence* (New York: Crown Books, 1999).

shots, one neck, and three upper torso). This is unprecedented marksmanship for a boy who only fired a .22 caliber rifle once at a summer camp.

The typical response in firing a gun is to fire at the target until it drops. Carneal instead moved from victim to victim just as he had learned in the violent video games he played.

The goal in these games is to rack up the "highest score" by moving quickly. Grossman points out that many of the games (such as "House of the Dead" or "Goldeneye" or "Turok") give bonus points for headshots.[186]

Does that mean that anyone who plays these games will be a killer? Of course not. But Grossman says that the kind of training we give to soldiers (operant conditioning, desensitization, etc.) is what we are also giving to our kids through many of these violent video games.

Ironically, the U.S. Marine Corps licensed one of these popular video games ("Doom") to train their combat fire teams in tactics and to rehearse combat actions of killing.[187] The video game manufacturers certainly know these are killing simulators. In fact the advertising for one game ("Quake II" that is produced by the same manufacturer as "Doom"), says: "We took what was killer, and made it mass murder."

---

[186] Statement of Lieutenant Colonel Dave Grossman, given before the New York State Legislature, October
1999, www.fradical.com/statement_of_lieutenant_colonel_dave_Grossman.htm

[187] Ibid.

Biblical Discernment

If we look back at the list of different types of video games, it is pretty easy to see that it is possible to find acceptable games as well as questionable and even dangerous video games in just about any category. That is why parental direction and discernment are so important.

The latest controversy over "Grand Theft Auto" demonstrates that the video game industry has not been effective at self-regulation. And children cannot be expected to exercise good judgment unless parents use discernment and teach it to their kids.

Paul tells us in Philippians 4:8, "Finally, brothers, whatever is true, whatever is noble, whatever is right, whatever is pure, whatever is lovely, whatever is admirable—if anything is excellent or praiseworthy—think about such things." We should focus on what is positive and helpful to our Christian walk.

As Christians, we should develop discernment in our lives. Parents need to determine the possible benefits to playing videos and whether those benefits outweigh the negatives. Many of the games available today raise little or no concern. As one commentator put it, "The majority of video games on the best-seller list contain no more bloodshed than a game of Risk."[188]

But even good, constructive games played for long periods of time can be detrimental. Over the last few years, I have been compiling statistics for my teen talk on media use. The number of hours young people spend watching TV, listening to music, surfing the Internet, going to movies, etc. is huge and increasing every year. Young people spend entirely too much time in front of a screen (TV screen, computer screen, movie screen).

---

[188] Steven Johnson, *Discover*, 41

Even good video games can be bad if young people are staying indoors and not going outdoors for exercise. Obesity is already a problem among many young people. And good video games can be bad if they take priority over responsibilities at home and schoolwork.

Parents should understand the potential dangers of video games and make sure they approve of the video games that come into their home. They may conclude that the drawbacks outweigh the benefits. If their children do play video games, they should also set time limits and monitor attitudes and behaviors that appear. They should also watch for signs of addiction. The dangers of video games are real, and parents need to exercise discernment.

CHAPTER 17 Media and Discernment

We live in the midst of a media storm. Every day we are confronted by more media messages than a previous generation could even imagine.

Media Exposure

For example, more homes have TV sets (98 percent) than have indoor plumbing. In the average home the television set is on for more than six hours a day. Children spend more time watching television than in any other activity except sleep.[189] Nearly half of elementary school children and 60 percent of adolescents have television sets in their bedrooms.[190]

But that is just the beginning of the media exposure we encounter. The *Journal of the American Medical Association* estimates that the average teenager listens to 10,500 hours of music during their teen years.[191] Families are watching more movies than every before since they can now watch them on cable and satellite and rent or buy movies.

The amount of media exposure continues to increase every year. Recent studies of media usage reveal that people spend more than double the time with media than they think they do. This amounts to nearly twelve

---

[189] Huston and Wright, University of Kansas, "Television and Socialization of Young Children."

[190] E.H. Woodard and N. Gridina, *Media in the Home: The Fifth Annual Survey of Parents and Children 2000* (Philadelphia, PA: The Annenberg Public Policy Center of the University of Pennsylvania, 2000).

[191] Elizabeth F. Brown and William R. Hendee, "Adolescents and Their Music: Insights Into the Health of Adolescents," *The Journal of the American Medical Association* 262 (September 22-29, 1989): 1659.

hours a day total. And because of media multitasking, summing all media use by medium results in a staggering fifteen hours per day.[192]

Student use of the Internet has been increasing to all-time levels. A study done at the University of Massachusetts at Amherst found the following:[193]

- Nearly 90 percent of the students access the Internet every day.
- Students spent over ten hours per week using IM (instant messaging).
- Those same students spent over twenty-eight hours per week on the Internet.
- Nearly three-fourths spent more time online than they intended.

In addition to concerns about the quantity of media, input is even greater concerns about the quality of media input. For example, the average child will witness over 200,000 acts of violence on television, including 16,000 murders before he or she is 18 years old. And consider that the average child views 30,000 commercials each year.

A study of adolescents (ages 12-17) showed that watching sex on TV influences teens to have sex. Youths were more likely to initiate intercourse as well as other sexual activities.[194]

---

[192] Robert A. Papper, et. al., "Middletown Media Studies," *International Digital Media & Arts Association Journal*, Vol. 1, No. 1, Spring 2004, 5.

[193] Gary D. Malaney, "Student Internet Use at UMass Amherst," *Student Affairs Online*, Vol. 5, No. 1, Jan. 2004.

[194] Rebecca Collins, et. al., "Watching Sex on Television Predicts Adolescent Initiation of Sexual Behavior," *Pediatrics*, Vol. 114 (3), September 2004.

Over 1000 studies (including reports from the Surgeon General's office and the National Institute of Mental Health) "point overwhelmingly to a causal connection between media violence and aggressive behavior in some children."[195]

To put it simply, we are awash in media exposure, and there is a critical need for Christians to exercise discernment. Never has a generation been so tempted to conform to this world (Rom. 12:1-2) because of the growing influence of the proliferating forms of media.

Biblical Discernment

Although the Bible does not provide specific instructions about media (you can't find a verse dealing with television, computers, or DVDs), it nevertheless provides broad principles concerning discernment.

For example, the apostle Paul in 2 Timothy 2:22 instructs us to "Flee from youthful lusts." We should stay away from anything (including media) that inflames our lust. Paul also goes on to say that in addition to fleeing from these things, we should also "pursue righteousness, faith, love and peace." We should replace negative influences in our life with those things which are positive.

Paul says in Colossians 3:8, "But now you must rid yourselves of all such things as these: anger, rage, malice, slander, and filthy language from your lips." Now, does that mean you could never read something that has anger or rage or slander in it? No. After all, the Bible has stories of people who manifest those traits in their lives.

What Paul is saying is that we need to rid ourselves of such things. If the input into our lives (such as through media) manifests these traits, then a wise and discerning

---

[195] Joint Statement on the Impact of Entertainment Violence on Children, American Academy of Pediatrics, 26 July 2000.

Christian would re-evaluate what is an influence in his or her life.

Paul tells us in Philippians 4:8, "Finally, brothers, whatever is true, whatever is noble, whatever is right, whatever is pure, whatever is lovely, whatever is admirable—if anything is excellent or praiseworthy—think about such things." We should focus on what is positive and helpful to our Christian walk.

We are also admonished in Romans 13:13 to "behave decently as in the daytime, not in orgies and drunkenness, not in sexual immorality and debauchery, not in dissension and jealousy."

As Christians, we should develop discernment in our lives. We can do this in three ways: stop, listen, and look. Stop what you are doing long enough to evaluate the media exposure in your life. Most of us just allow media to wash over us every day without considering the impact it is having on us.

Second, we should listen. That is, we should give attention to what is being said. Is it true or false? And what is the message various media are bringing into our lives?

Finally, we should look. We need to look at the consequences of media in our lives. We should rid ourselves of influences that are negative and think on those things that are positive.

Worldview of the News Media

Of all the forms of media, the news media have become a primary shaper of our perspective on the world. Also, the rules of journalism have changed in the last few decades. It used to be assumed that reporters or broadcasters would attempt to look at events through the eyes of the average reader or viewer. It was also assumed that they would not use their positions in the media to influence the thinking of the nation but merely to report the facts of an event objectively. Things have changed dramatically in the news business.

The fact that people in the media are out of step with the American people should be a self-evident statement. But for anyone who does not believe it, there is abundant empirical evidence to support it.

Probably the best-known research on media bias was first published in the early 1980s by professors Robert Lichter and Stanley Rothman. Their research, published in the journal *Public Opinion*[196] and later collected in the book *The Media Elite*,[197] demonstrated that reporters and broadcasters in the prestige media differ in significant ways from their audiences.

They surveyed 240 editors and reporters of the media elite—*New York Times*, *Washington Post*, *Time*, *Newsweek*, ABC, NBC, and CBS. Their research confirmed what many suspected for a long time: the media elite are liberal, secular, and humanistic.

People have always complained about the liberal bias in the media. But what was so surprising is how liberal members of the media actually were. When asked to describe their own political persuasion, 54 percent of the media elite described themselves as left of center. Only 19 percent described themselves as conservative. When asked who they voted for in presidential elections, more than 80 percent of them always voted for the Democratic candidate.

Media personnel is also very secular in their outlook. The survey found that 86 percent of the media elite

---

[196] S. Robert Lichter and Stanley Rothman, "Media and Business Elites," *Public Opinion*, (October-November 1981): 42-46.

[197] S. Robert Lichter, Stanley Rothman, and Linda S. Lichter, *The Media Elite* (New York: Adler and Adler, 1986).

seldom or never attend religious services. In fact, 50 percent of them have no religious affiliation at all.

This bias is especially evident when the secular press tries to cover religious events or religious issues. Most of them do not attend church, nor do they even know people who do. Instead, they live in a secularized world and therefore tend to underestimate the significance of religious values in American lives and to paint anyone with Christian convictions as a "fundamentalist."

Finally, they also found that the news media was humanistic in their outlook on social issues. Over 90 percent of the media elite support a woman's so-called "right to abortion" while only 24 percent agreed or strongly agreed that "homosexuality is wrong."

For a time, members of the media elite argued against these studies. They suggested that the statistical sample was too small. But when Robert Lichter began to enumerate the 240 members of the news media interviewed, that tactic was quickly set aside. Others tried to argue that, though the media might be liberal, secular, and humanistic, it did not affect the way the press covered the news. Later studies by a variety of media watchdogs began to erode the acceptance of that view.

A second significant study on media bias was a 1996 survey conducted by the Freedom Forum and the Roper Center.[198] Their survey of 139 Washington bureau chiefs and congressional correspondents showed a decided preference for liberal candidates and causes.

The journalists were asked for whom they voted in the 1992 election. The results were these: 89 percent said Bill Clinton, 7 percent George Bush, 2 percent Ross Perot. But in the election, 43 percent of Americans voted for Clinton and 37 percent voted for Bush.

---

[198] S. Robert Lichter, "Consistently Liberal: But Does It Matter?" *Media Critic* (Summer 1996): 26-39.

Another question they were asked was, "What is your current political affiliation?" Fifty percent said they were Democrats, 4 percent Republicans. In answer to the question, "How do you characterize your political orientation?" 61 percent said they were liberal or moderately liberal, and 9 percent were conservative or moderately conservative.

The reporters were also asked about their attitudes toward their jobs. They said they see their coverage of news events as a mission. No less than 92 percent agreed with the statement, "Our role is to educate the public." And 62 percent agreed with the statement, "Our role is sometimes to suggest potential solutions to social problems."

A more recent survey by the Pew Research Center further confirms the liberal bias in the media. They interviewed 547 media professionals (print, TV, and radio) and asked them to identify their political perspective. They found that 34 percent were liberal and only 7 percent were conservative. This compares to 20 percent of Americans who identify themselves as liberal and 33 percent who define themselves as conservative.[199]

It is also worth questioning whether a majority of media professionals who labeled themselves as moderate in the survey really deserve that label. John Leo, writing for *U.S. News and World Report*, says that it has been his experience "that liberal journalists tend to think of themselves as representing the mainstream, so in these self-identification polls, moderate usually translates to liberal. On the few social questions asked in the survey, most of the moderates sounded fairly liberal."[200]

---

[199] "Survey: Liberals dominate news outlets: Far higher number in press than in general population," *WorldNetDaily*, 24 May 2004.

[200] John Leo, "Liberal media? I'm shocked!" *U.S. News and World Report*, 7 June 2004, 12.

Once again, we see the need for Christians to exercise discernment in their consumption of media.

Biblical Principles and Application

Christians must address the influence of the media in society. It can be a dangerous influence that can conform us to the world (Rom. 12:2). Therefore we should do all we can to protect against its influence and to use the media for good.

Christians should strive to apply the following two passages to their lives as they seek discernment concerning the media: Philippians 4:8, which we quoted above, and Colossians 3:2–5: "Set your minds on things above, not on earthly things. For you died, and your life is now hidden with Christ in God. When Christ, who is your life, appears, then you also will appear with him in glory. Put to death, therefore, whatever belongs to your earthly nature: sexual immorality, impurity, lust, evil desires and greed, which is idolatry."

Here are some suggestions for action.

First, control the quantity and quality of media input. Parents should set down guidelines and help select television programs at the start of the week and watch only those. Parents should also set down guidelines for movies, music, and other forms of media. Families should also evaluate the location of their television set so that it is not so easy to just sit and watch TV for long hours.

Second, watch TV with children. One way to encourage discussion with children is to watch television with them. The plots and actions of the programs provide a natural context for discussion. The discussion could focus on how cartoon characters or TV characters could solve their problems without resorting to violence. What are the consequences of violence? TV often ignores the consequences. What are the consequences of promiscuous sex in real life?

Third, set a good example. Parents should not be guilty of saying one thing and doing another. Neither adults nor children should spend long periods of time in front of a video display (television, video game, computer). Parents can teach their children by example that there are better ways to spend time.

Fourth, work to establish broadcaster guidelines. No TV or movie producer wants to unilaterally disarm all the actors on their screens for fear that viewers will watch other programs and movies. Yet many of these TV and movie producers would like to tone down the violence, even though they do not want to be the first to do so. National standards would be able to achieve what individuals would not do by themselves in a competitive market.

Fifth, make your opinions known. Writing letters to programs, networks, and advertisers can make a difference over time. A single letter may not make a difference, but large numbers of letters can even change editorial policy. Consider joining with other like-minded people in seeking to make a difference in the media.

While the media has a tremendous potential for good, it can also have some very negative effects. Christians need wisdom and discernment to utilize the positive aspects of media and to guard against its negative effects.

Bibliography

Andrews, Edward D. *For As I Think – In My Heart – So I Am: Combining Biblical Counseling with Cognitive Behavioral Therapy [Second Edition]* Cambridge, OH: Christian Publishing House, 2016.

Anderson, Kerby. Christian Ethics in Plain Language. Thomas Nelson, 2005.

Anderson, Kerby. *Genetic Engineering*. Grand Rapids: Zondervan, 1982.

Anderson, Kerby. *Signs of Warning, Signs of Hope*. Chicago: Moody Press, 1994.

Ellul, Jacques, *The Technological Society*. New York: Vintage, 1964.

Friedman, Thomas. *The World is Flat: A Brief History of the Twenty-First Century*. New York: Farrar, Straus and Giroux, 2005.

Jones, Landon. *Great Expectations: America and the Baby Boom Generation*. New York: Ballantine, 1980.

Lewis, C. S. *The Abolition of Man*. New York: Macmillan, 1947.

Lichter, Robert, Stanley Rothman, and Linda S. Lichter, *The Media Elite*. New York: Adler and Adler, 1986.

Raasch, Charles. "Big Data transforms our lives and lifestyles." *USA Today*, 13 December 2012.

Rainer, Thom and Jess Rainer. *The Millennials: Connecting to America's Largest Generation*. Nashville, B&H Publishing Group, 2011.

Smolen, Rick and Erwitt, Jennifer. *The Human Face of Big Data*. Against All Odds Productions, 2012.

Swenson, Richard Swenson. *Margin: How to Create the Emotional, Physical, Financial, and Time Reserves You Need*. Colorado Springs: NavPress, 1992.

Terlizzese, Lawrence. Into the Void: The Coming Transhuman Transformation. Cambridge, OH: Christian Publishing House, 2016.

Other Books by Kerby Anderson

CHRISTIAN PUBLISHING
HOUSE & PROBE MINISTRIES

CHRISTIANS AND ECONOMICS
A Biblical Point of View

KERBY ANDERSON

For the love of money is a root of all sorts of evil.—1 Tim. 6:10, NASB.